The
de' MEDICI
Kitchen

The
de' MEDICI
Kitchen

LORENZA DE' MEDICI

CollinsPublishersSanFrancisco
A Division of HarperCollins*Publishers*

This edition first published in USA 1992 by

Collins Publishers San Francisco
1160 Battery Street
San Francisco CA 94111

Created and produced by Weldon Owen Inc.
814 Montgomery Street, San Francisco, CA 94133
Phone: (415) 291 0100, Fax: (415) 291 8841

Weldon Owen Inc.
President: John Owen
Publisher: Jane Fraser
Senior Editor: Anne Dickerson
Editorial Assistant: Amy Morton
Marketing Director: Dawn Low
Copy Editor: Sharon Silva
Proofreader: Kathryn Wright
Text Authors and Recipe Translators: Michael Dunkley
    and Anthony Dunkley
Additional Text Author: Shelley Handler
Production: Stephanie Sherman, Mick Bagnato
Designer: John Bull, The Book Design Company
Food Photographer: Peter Johnson
Food Stylist: Janice Baker
Author Photographer: Dan Escabar

Produced in association with KQED
Vice President, Television Productions: Marjorie Poore
Executive Producer: Peter L. Stein

Production by Mandarin Offset, Hong Kong
Printed in Hong Kong

A Weldon Owen/KQED Production

Library of Congress Cataloging-in-Publication Data:

De' Medici Stucchi, Lorenza, date.
  The de' Medici kitchen / Lorenza de' Medici .
  p.   cm.
  ". . . as presented on the 13-part television series The de' Medici
  kitchen"--CIP p. 8.
  Includes Index.
  ISBN 0-00-255150-0
  1. Cookery, Italian. 2. Cookery--Italy. 3. Food habits--Italy.
  I. De' Medici kitchen (Television program) II. Title.
  TX723.D4257 1992
  641.5945--dc20   92-26386

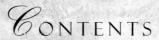

Contents

INTRODUCTION

For many years, I have been both hostess and cooking teacher in my eleventh-century abbey in Tuscany, Badia a Coltibuono, and now thanks to KQED and my publisher I will be sharing our centuries-old heritage of cuisine and hospitality with the American public.

In this book and television series, I present Italian cooking as it has been developed over the centuries in the kitchens of Italian families.

It is a cuisine both uncomplicated and refined and whose clean, balanced tastes depend on fresh ingredients, simply but knowingly prepared. This food celebrates the connection between the glorious produce from the land and the culinary skills passed from generation to generation in Italy.

Each menu expresses my approach to cooking and entertaining: meals that are simple, attractive, and generous with a minimum of last-minute preparation and fuss.

I hope I have given a unique and memorable experience of the tastes of Italy in *The de' Medici Kitchen*.

Lorenza di Medici

Menus

As presented on the 13-part television series *The de' Medici Kitchen*

An Autumn Menu

Polenta ai funghi 31
Frittata arrotolata 46
Indivia del Belgio alle noci 101
Crostata di uva 108

A Family Lunch

Piadina al prosciutto 49
Polpettone alle uova sode 71
Spinaci agli amaretti 101
Frutta fresca

Summer Buffet

Linguine alla peperonata 24
Sformato di prosciutto 54
Pesche agli amaretti 114

Roman Lunch

Gnocchi di patate al pomodoro 22
Fricassea d'agnello 82
Fagiolini alle nocciole 94
Ricotta al miele 123

Lunch from Liguria

Insalata di baccalà e fagioli 40
Coniglio ai capperi e basilico 79
Porri allo zafferano 95
Torta di nocciole 116

A Piedmontese Feast

Tortelli di formaggio e burro di
  tartufo 25
Piccioni al ginepro 65
Finocchi all'acciuga 89
Torta della nonna 118

Winter Table for Two

Bruschetta alle olive 44
Costolette di maiale alle prugne 83
Involtini di lattuga 90
Albicocche alla grappa 107
Caffè con grappa 110

Coltibuono Favorites

Risotto alle quaglie 35
Insalata di Coltibuono 35
Tiramisù 112

Italian Spice Box

Bucatini all'amatriciana 14
Manzo ai chiodi di garofano 81
Broccoli alla salsiccia 92
Moro in camicia 111

Spring Menu

Anello di riso primavera 15
Pesce alle erbe 67
Patate arrosto 87
Semifreddo di fragole al
  torrone 117

Foods of the Po Valley

Passatelli alla romagnola 29
Carpaccio al balsamico 57
Melanzane all'agro 97
Panna cotta al caffè 122

Picnic in the Vineyards

Schiacciata di formaggio 55
Ciambella alla salsiccia e formaggio 45
Macedonia di arance 123

Flavors of Tuscany

Panzanella 18
Pomodori ripieni 51
Polenta alla griglia 41
Peperoni alla marinara 94
Pinolata 120
Cappuccino 110

I PRIMI

First Courses

Traditionally a *primo piatto* comprised the whole meal for all but Italy's well-to-do classes. Even today these dishes, which are usually based on pasta or rice and embellished in Italian style, are often the most substantial courses on a menu.

The best-known *primi piatti* are the pastas, available in scores of shapes and sizes—in narrow ribbons, thick rods, fine nests, as filled rounds or squares. The Italians have been eating pasta for centuries, since long before Marco Polo's legendary journey to China in the mid-1200s. Indeed, the once-popular belief that this famed traveler brought pasta-making skills back to Italy has few adherents today. One proof of the impossibility is a cookbook published some five years before Marco Polo's return that includes recipes for both *vermicelli* and *tortelli*.

By the late eighteenth century, pasta had become the staple food of Campania, the region surrounding Naples. It was common in those days for the flour to be ground in large granite hand mills and for the dough to be kneaded by barefoot men and children stomping it in rough wooden troughs. Once cut, the pasta strips were hung to dry in the south's bright sun and soft sea breezes.

Northerners are the rice eaters of Italy and they have turned this versatile grain into countless *primi piatti*, from creamy *risotto* with roasted quail to delicate rice molds flecked with springtime vegetables. The great Po River valley is Italy's premier rice-growing area, and it is there that the exceptional short-grain Arborio, Vialone nano, and Carnaroli varieties are harvested.

Italians have long known that they grow extraordinary rice. In the eighteenth century they sought to maintain a monopoly on it by ruling its export a capital crime. In 1787 Thomas Jefferson defied the law and smuggled out rice seeds he later planted at his Virginia home of Monticello. Those seeds launched the American rice industry.

Both northern and central Italians prepare first courses of *gnocchi*, the small light dumplings made of plain wheat flour, semolina, or potato, depending upon the region. Two *gnocchi* recipes are offered in these pages, *gnocchetti alle verze* (with cheese) and *gnocchi di patate al pomodoro* (with tomato sauce), but there are many other ways to serve these tasty dumplings, including topped with *pesto*, Genoese style. Each of these dishes, as with so many of the *primi piatti*, is hearty enough to stand alone as a meal.

Crema di Zucca agli Amaretti

Pumpkin Soup with Macaroons

Pumpkin is often served in fall and winter in Lombardy, the Veneto, and Sicily. It is used as a filling for *ravioli*, for enhancing various soups, and in *risotto*. Pumpkin is also puréed or sliced and sautéed and served as an accompaniment to meats.

¼ cup (2 oz/60 g) unsalted butter
1 large onion, thinly sliced
2½ lb (1.2 kg) pumpkin, peeled, seeded, and cut into small cubes
1 teaspoon freshly grated nutmeg
salt and freshly ground pepper
12 *amaretti* (imported Italian macaroons)
6 cups (48 fl oz/1.5 l) light meat stock
¾ cup (3 oz/90 g) freshly grated Parmesan cheese

Preheat a broiler (griller). In a large saucepan over medium heat, melt half of the butter. Add the onion and cook, stirring, until translucent, about 3 minutes. Add the pumpkin, cover, and cook, stirring occasionally, until the pumpkin is soft, about 10 minutes.
▓ Sprinkle the pumpkin with nutmeg and season to taste with salt and pepper. Add the *amaretti* and beat with a hand blender. Blend until creamy.
▓ Pour the pumpkin puree into a deep saucepan, add the stock, and bring to a boil. Pour the soup into a heated flameproof serving bowl. Cut the remaining butter into thin slices and float them on the soup. Sprinkle the Parmesan cheese over the top. Place the soup under the broiler until the cheese is deep gold, about 5 minutes. Serve immediately.

Serves 6

From top to bottom: Pumpkin Soup with Macaroons, Risotto Primavera Mold, Bucatini with Spicy Tomato and Pancetta Sauce

Bucatini all'Amatriciana

Bucatini with Spicy Tomato and Pancetta Sauce

A specialty of Amatrice, a small city in the region of Lazio, this pasta dish is now popular throughout Italy. It is important to toss the hot *bucatini* with the sauce in the frying pan so that the noodles will "drink up" the sauce. *Bucatini* are long, hollow pasta rods that are slightly larger than spaghetti.

6 oz (180 g) *pancetta* or bacon, diced
1 onion, thinly sliced
2 lb (900 g) very ripe plum (egg) tomatoes, peeled, or canned with their liquid
pinch of finely crushed dried red chili
salt
1¼ lb (600 g) *bucatini* or spaghetti
¾ cup (3 oz/90 g) freshly grated *romano* cheese

Put the *pancetta* in a large frying pan over medium heat and cook, stirring occasionally, until crisp and transparent, about 5 minutes. Add the onion and continue to cook, stirring, until the onion is barely golden, about 5 minutes. Add the tomatoes and chili. Sprinkle the mixture with salt to taste and cook, uncovered, until thickened, about 10 minutes.

▣ Meanwhile, bring a large saucepan of salted water to a boil, add the *bucatini*, and cook until *al dente*. Drain the pasta and add it to the frying pan holding the sauce. Stir for 2 minutes, pour onto a platter, and serve immediately, accompanied with the grated cheese.

Serves 6

Anello di Riso Primavera

Risotto Primavera Mold

6 cups (48 fl oz/1.5 l) vegetable stock
½ cup (4 oz/120 g) unsalted butter
3 green (spring) onions, chopped
2¼ cups (14 oz/ 420 g) Arborio or Vialone nano rice
1 cup (4 oz/120 g) shelled green peas
4 oz (120 g) asparagus tips, diced
4 oz (120 g) string beans, diced
4 oz (120 g) young carrots, diced
1 tablespoon minced fresh chives
1 tablespoon minced fresh flat-leaf (Italian) parsley
salt
2 tablespoons extra-virgin olive oil
3 tomatoes, peeled, seeded, and diced

Preheat an oven to 400°F (200°C). Pour the stock into a saucepan and bring to a simmer over very low heat. Butter a 9-in (23-cm) ring mold with 1 tablespoon of the butter and set aside.

Melt half of the remaining butter in a heavy saucepan over medium heat. Add the onions and cook, stirring, until translucent, about 3 minutes. Add the rice and cook, stirring, for about 2 minutes. Add about 2 cups (500 ml) of the simmering stock and continue to stir. Continue adding stock, a ladleful at a time, allowing most of the liquid to be absorbed before adding more stock. Make sure that the rice is always covered with a thin layer of stock. After 9 minutes, add the peas, asparagus, beans, and carrots and cook for 3 minutes, allowing the mixture to become a little drier.

Remove the rice from the heat and add the remaining butter, the chives, parsley, and salt. Stir well and pour the mixture into the prepared mold. Transfer the mold to the preheated oven and bake for 5 minutes.

While the mold is in the oven, heat the oil in a frying pan over medium-high heat and add the tomatoes. Sauté until heated through, a few minutes. When the mold is ready, run a knife blade around the edges to loosen it, then invert onto a platter. Fill the hollow center with the tomatoes and serve immediately.

Serves 6

Tagliatelle Verdi agli Asparagi

Green Noodles with Asparagus

Pasta may be colored with puréed vegetables such as spinach, beets, or tomatoes, with the purée substituting for one of the eggs. If the dough is too dry, add an extra egg yolk. To flavor a pasta with fresh herbs, add a few tablespoons of very finely chopped parsley, sage, rosemary, thyme, or basil; do not reduce the number of eggs.

10 oz (300 g) spinach
2⅓ cups (10 oz/300 g) all-purpose (plain) flour
2 extra-large eggs
2 lb (900 g) asparagus tips
½ cup (4 oz/120 g) unsalted butter
salt and freshly ground pepper
¾ cup (3 oz/90 g) freshly grated Parmesan cheese

Have a large bowl of ice water ready. Bring a large saucepan of salted water to a boil and add the spinach. Blanch for 1 minute, then remove with a slotted spoon to the ice water to halt the cooking. Drain and squeeze as dry as possible, then purée in a food processor.

▨ Using the flour, eggs, and spinach, make the pasta dough by following the step-by-step instructions on page 19, adding the spinach to the well. When the dough has been rolled out, cut it into noodles about ⅜ in (1 cm) wide. Set aside on a floured work surface and cover with a towel while you prepare the sauce.

▨ Ready another large bowl of ice water. Bring a large saucepan filled with salted water to a boil and add the asparagus. Blanch for 2 minutes, then remove with a slotted spoon to the ice water to halt the cooking. Drain and dice.

▨ Bring a large saucepan of salted water to a boil, add the noodles, and cook until they rise to the surface, about 2 minutes. Meanwhile, melt the butter in a frying pan, add the asparagus, and heat through. Drain the noodles and arrange on a heated platter. Pour the asparagus over the top, toss well, and season to taste with salt and pepper. Sprinkle with the cheese and serve immediately.

Serves 6

From top to bottom: Bread Salad with Tomato, Green Noodles with Asparagus

Panzanella
Bread Salad with Tomato

In Tuscany leftover bread is mixed with vine-ripened tomatoes, onions, and deep green olive oil to create this simple yet delicious salad.

8 oz (240 g) week-old, coarse-textured bread
3 large ripe tomatoes, peeled and cut into small cubes
2 small red (Spanish) onions, sliced paper-thin
½ cup (½ oz/15 g) whole fresh basil leaves
2 tablespoons red wine vinegar
salt
⅓ cup (3 fl oz/90 ml) extra-virgin olive oil
freshly ground pepper

In a bowl soak the bread in water to cover for a few minutes. Squeeze dry and crumble into a large mixing bowl.

▣ Add the tomatoes, onions, and basil to the bread.

▣ In a small bowl, whisk the vinegar with a pinch of salt until the salt is dissolved. Whisk in the olive oil. Add the dressing to the salad, toss, season to taste with the salt and pepper, and serve.

Serves 6

MAKING PASTA

1. Heap the flour in a bowl or on a work surface and make a well in the center. Break the eggs into the well. Using a fork, lightly beat the eggs. Then, with a circular motion, gradually pull the flour into the well. Continue until all the flour is incorporated

2. If using a food processor, combine the flour and eggs in the work bowl fitted with the metal blade. Pulse briefly a few times to combine the ingredients, then process using long pulses just until the dough forms a ball around the blade, about 1 minute.

3. On a floured work surface, knead the dough, using the palms and heels of your hands. Push it down and away and turn repeatedly until it is smooth, elastic, and not too soft, at least 5 minutes.

4. To roll out the dough on a floured work surface, flatten the ball of dough with the palm of your hand and roll out with a flour-dusted rolling pin to the desired thickness (about $\frac{1}{32}$ in [1 mm] thick for pasta ribbons such as *tagliatelle* and *fettuccine* and $\frac{1}{64}$ in [0.5 mm] for filled pastas). Always roll away from you and rotate the disk of dough as it becomes thinner and thinner.

5. If using a hand-crank pasta machine to roll the dough, divide it into 6 equal portions. Working with 1 portion at a time, start with the rollers at the widest setting and pass the dough through them. Continue to pass the dough through the rollers, progressively adjusting the rollers to a narrower setting until it is the desired thickness. Always dust the dough with flour before putting it through the next setting.

Spaghetti ai Piselli e Scampi

Spaghetti with Peas and Shrimp

This colorful springtime pasta is quick to prepare. The flavors of the shrimp and the lightly cooked vegetables remain separate, yet blend together. The two nontraditional ingredients, curry and ketchup (tomato sauce), are now commonly used in Italian homes. The dish may also be made with *taglierini* or *linguine*.

1 lb (450 g) spaghetti
3 tablespoons extra-virgin olive oil
10 oz (300 g) shrimp (prawns), peeled and deveined
scant 1 cup (7 fl oz/210 ml) heavy (double) cream
1 tablespoon ketchup (tomato sauce)
1 tablespoon curry powder
1 large red bell pepper (capsicum), seeded, deribbed, and diced
1 cup (4 oz/120 g) small shelled green peas
salt

Bring a large saucepan filled with salted water to a boil. Add the spaghetti and cook until *al dente*.

▣ Meanwhile, heat the oil in a frying pan over medium heat. Add the shrimp and cook, turning once, for 2 minutes.

▣ Pour the cream into a large frying pan, stir in the ketchup and curry powder, and bring to a boil. Add the shrimp, pepper, and peas and cook for 2 minutes. Drain the spaghetti and add it to the frying pan holding the sauce. Stir over medium heat for 1 minute. Season to taste with salt, arrange on a heated platter, and serve immediately.

Serves 6

Gnocchi di Patate al Pomodoro

Potato Dumplings in Tomato Sauce

Potato *gnocchi* originated in Italy in the late 1700s and quickly became popular. Even Escoffier included recipes for them in his works, and at carnival time each year in Verona, a *Papà del gnocco* ("Father of the *gnocco*") is elected.

2 lb (900 g) plum (egg) tomatoes, peeled, seeded, and chopped
salt
2½ lb (1.2 kg) boiling potatoes
1¾ cups (7 oz/210 g) all-purpose (plain) flour
2 large egg yolks, or 1 whole large egg if the mashed potatoes are very dry
freshly ground pepper
6 tablespoons (3 fl oz/90 ml) extra-virgin olive oil
½ cup (2 oz/60 g) freshly grated Parmesan cheese

Place the tomatoes in a colander, sprinkle them with a little salt, and set aside to drain for about 30 minutes.

▦ Boil the unpeeled potatoes in water to cover until tender. Drain and peel them. Put the potatoes through a ricer or mash them by hand until very smooth. To make the *gnocchi*, follow the step-by-step instructions on the facing page, using the potatoes, flour, and eggs.

▦ Set the *gnocchi* aside on a board while you make the sauce.

▦ Place the drained tomatoes in a saucepan and cook over low heat for about 10 minutes. Season to taste with salt and pepper, add the oil, and keep warm.

▦ To cook the *gnocchi*, bring a large saucepan of salted water to a boil and drop in the *gnocchi*, a few at a time. As soon as they rise to the surface, after about 3 minutes, lift them out with a slotted spoon and place on a heated platter. When all the *gnocchi* are cooked, spoon the tomato sauce over the top, sprinkle with the Parmesan, and serve immediately.

Serves 6

From top to bottom: Potato Dumplings in Tomato Sauce, Tortelli with Cheese and Truffle Butter, Linguine with Bell Peppers

1. Heap the mashed potatoes on a board, add half of the flour, and make a well in the center. Drop the egg yolks or the whole egg into the well.

Knead the mixture into a smooth, firm dough.

2. Coat a work surface and your hands with flour. Break the dough into large pieces and, using the palms of your hands, roll each piece into a log about ⅜ in (1 cm) in diameter.

3. Cut the logs into 1¼-in (3-cm) lengths. Gently roll each piece over the prongs of a fork, pressing lightly with the thumb to make the characteristic ridges.

Linguine alla Peperonata

Linguine with Bell Peppers

Pasta should always be cooked *al dente*, but it is difficult to give exact cooking times because of differences among brands. There are, however, two things that are forbidden when cooking pasta: you must never halt the cooking by rinsing pasta in cold water (it is enough to put it in a cold bowl and mix in a little oil or melted butter so that it does not stick) and – this is even worse – you must never half-cook pasta in advance, drain it, and then finish the cooking just before serving.

10 oz (300 g) tomatoes, peeled, seeded, and diced
salt
3 bell peppers (capsicums), a mixture of red and yellow
6 tablespoons (3 fl oz/90 ml) extra-virgin olive oil
1 onion, sliced
a pinch of finely crushed dried red chili
1 handful fresh basil leaves, torn into pieces
1¼ lb (600 g) *linguine*

Place the tomatoes in a colander, sprinkle them with a little salt, and set them aside to drain for 30 minutes. Preheat an oven to 350°F (180°C).

▨ Arrange the peppers on a baking pan and place in the preheated oven for 20 minutes. Remove from the oven, wrap in aluminum foil, and set aside for 20 minutes. Unwrap, cut in half lengthwise, peel, derib, and cut into long, thin strips.

▨ In a frying pan over low heat, warm the oil. Add the onion and cook, stirring, until translucent, about 3 minutes. Add the bell peppers and tomatoes, cover, and cook for 5 minutes. Season to taste with salt and sprinkle with the chili and basil.

▨ Meanwhile, bring a large saucepan of salted water to a boil, add the *linguine* and cook until *al dente*.

▨ Drain the *linguine* and transfer to a heated platter. Pour the pepper sauce over the top, toss, and serve at once.

Serves 6

In recent years, fresh pasta has taken precedence over dried, in the belief, perhaps, that if something is fresh it is better. Fresh pasta does work best with light sauces and fragile ingredients. Dried pasta is, however, equally important. Usually made of high-protein semolina, it stands up well to heftier ingredients such as sausage or eggplant. Its rough surface holds sauce tenaciously, as do the ridges, holes, and swirls of the various shapes. At the tiny Martelli pasta factory near Pisa, production moves at a gentle pace. Extruded quite slowly, the pasta emerges rough and slightly porous, ensuring that the sauce will cling to the pasta and not to the plate.

Tortelli di Formaggio e Burro di Tartufo

Tortelli with Cheese and Truffle Butter

3 oz (90 g) Gorgonzola cheese
3 oz (90 g) ricotta
1¼ cups (5 oz/150 g) freshly grated Parmesan cheese
1 egg
1¾ cups (7 oz/210 g) all-purpose (plain) flour
2 extra-large eggs
¼ cup (2 oz/60 g) unsalted butter, or
    ½ cup (4 oz/120 g) unsalted butter if not using truffle butter
¼ cup (2 oz/60 g) truffle butter, optional

To make the filling, combine the Gorgonzola, ricotta, ¾ cup (3 oz/90 g) Parmesan cheese and egg in a food processor fitted with the metal blade and process until smooth. Set aside.

▨ Using the flour and eggs, make the pasta dough by following the step-by-step instructions on page 19.

▨ When the dough has been rolled out, cut it into strips about 4 in (10 cm) wide, then follow the step-by-step instructions for making *ravioli* on page 33, cutting the *tortelli* into 2-in (5-cm) squares. Set the *tortelli* aside on a floured surface, or, if not cooking immediately, store covered with plastic wrap in the refrigerator for up to 6 hours.

▨ Bring a large saucepan of salted water to a boil. Melt the butter in a separate saucepan over low heat, add the truffle butter, and keep warm. If not using truffle butter, substitute ¼ cup (2 oz/60 g) melted butter. Reduce the water to a simmer and drop in the *tortelli*, a few at a time. As soon as they rise to the surface, in about 2 minutes, lift out with a slotted spoon and arrange on a heated serving platter. When all of the *tortelli* are cooked, sprinkle with the remaining Parmesan, spoon the truffle sauce over the top, and serve immediately.

Serves 6

A white truffle is a solid, pungent, subterranean fungus commonly found in Tuscany, Piedmont, and Marche. Since truffles are not visible above ground, they must be found with an acute sense of smell. Female pigs were often used because truffles give off an aroma that replicates the male pig's hormonal scent during mating season. Clever reasoning—but wresting the truffle from the bewildered sow was often an ordeal. Today, dogs are typically used to sniff out the elusive truffles. A good truffle dog is worth its weight in gold—as truffles may sell for as much as $3000 a kilo.

Lasagne al Pesto

Large Noodles with Pesto Sauce

In Liguria *lasagne* are typically served with *pesto* sauce, a combination of garlic, olive oil, fresh basil, pine nuts, and *pecorino romano* and Parmesan cheeses. Avoid buying *pesto* in jars, as it is always of poor quality. Basil cannot be kept under oil for more than a few days, even in the refrigerator, because it ferments. But *pesto* can be made in only a couple of minutes, so it is worth preparing it at the last moment.

2⅓ cups (10 oz/300 g) all-purpose (plain) flour
3 extra-large eggs
1 cup (1 oz/30 g) fresh basil leaves
salt
2 cloves garlic
2 tablespoons pine nuts
3 tablespoons freshly grated *pecorino romano* cheese
3 tablespoons freshly grated Parmesan cheese
½ cup (4 fl oz/120 ml) extra-virgin olive oil

Using the flour and eggs, make the pasta dough by following the step-by-step instructions on page 19. When the dough has been rolled out, cut it into 4-in (10-cm) squares. Set aside on a floured work surface and cover with a towel.

▣ To make the *pesto*, put the basil and salt (the salt will prevent the basil from turning black) into a food processor fitted with a metal blade. Process briefly, then add the garlic, pine nuts, and both cheeses. With the machine running, pour in the oil in a thin, steady stream and process until well incorporated.

▣ Bring a large saucepan filled with salted water to a boil and drop in the pasta squares, a few at a time. As soon as they rise to the surface, lift them out with a slotted spoon and arrange on a heated serving platter. Add 6 tablespoons of the pasta water to the *pesto* sauce and mix well. When all the squares are cooked, pour the *pesto* over the top and serve immediately.

Serves 6

Passatelli alla Romagnola

Bolognese Dumplings

Passatelli are part of the traditional cuisine of Emilia-Romagna, where they are made with a special utensil called a *passatelli* iron. The dough is generally a mixture of bread crumbs, eggs, Parmesan cheese, nutmeg, lemon zest, and beef marrow. In Italy beef marrow is considered essential to the dough because it creates the perfect softness. Substituting the same quantity of butter produces acceptable *passatelli*. The dough may be covered and refrigerated for up to three hours before cooking.

2 tablespoons unsalted butter, softened
1 cup (2 oz/60 g) soft fresh bread crumbs, made from coarse-textured bread with crusts
    removed
½ cup (2 oz/60 g) freshly grated Parmesan cheese
2 oz (60 g) *mortadella*, puréed
1 egg
1 teaspoon grated lemon zest
¼ teaspoon freshly grated nutmeg
salt and freshly ground pepper
2 cups (16 fl oz/480 ml) light meat stock

To make the dumplings, combine the butter, bread crumbs, cheese, *mortadella*, egg, lemon zest, and nutmeg in a mixing bowl. Sprinkle to taste with salt and pepper. Using your fingers, work the mixture until it is thoroughly blended. Alternatively, process it in a food processor fitted with the plastic blade. If the dough is too hard, soften it with a little of the stock, being careful not to make it too soft.

To cook the *passatelli*, bring the stock to a boil in a large saucepan. Turn the dough into a potato ricer, food mill, or sieve with large holes (to create short cylinders) and push it directly into the boiling stock. Cook until the *passatelli* rise to the surface, about 2 minutes, then ladle the stock and pasta into individual bowls and serve.

Serves 2

Clockwise from top left: Bolognese Dumplings, Polenta with Mushrooms, Noodles and Chick-Peas

Stracci e Ceci

Noodles and Chick-Peas

Chick-peas are among the few vegetables that are good even from the can, but the dried ones are better. *Stracci* are wide noodles about 2 in (5 cm) long.

1½ cups (10 oz/300 g) dried chick-peas (garbanzo beans)
9 tablespoons (4 fl oz/120 ml) extra-virgin olive oil
2 oz (60 g) chopped *pancetta* or bacon
3 tablespoons finely chopped fresh rosemary
3 cloves garlic, chopped
8 cups (64 fl oz/2 l) light meat stock
1¼ cups (5 oz/150 g) all-purpose (plain) flour
1 extra-large egg and 1 yolk
salt and freshly ground pepper

Soak the chick-peas in cold water to cover for about 12 hours. Drain and place in a deep saucepan. Add water to cover by 1¼ in (3 cm) and 1 tablespoon of the oil. Cover and simmer over very low heat for about 3 hours. Remove the pan from the heat, but do not drain the chick-peas.

◼ In a deep saucepan over medium heat, warm 2 tablespoons of the oil. Add the *pancetta*, rosemary, and garlic and cook, stirring frequently, until the *pancetta* is translucent, about 5 minutes. Add the stock and chick-peas with their liquid and cook over low heat for about 10 minutes.

◼ Using the flour and eggs, follow the step-by-step instructions for making pasta on page 19. When the dough has been rolled out, cut it into noodles about ¾ in (2 cm) wide and 2 in (5 cm) long. Set the noodles aside, covered with a cloth, until you are ready to cook them.

◼ Purée the chick-peas with one quick pass of a hand blender so that at least half the chick-peas remain whole. Add the noodles and cook until they rise to the surface, about 2 minutes. Season to taste with salt and pepper. Divide among 6 individual soup bowls, add 1 tablespoon oil to each bowl, and serve.

Serves 6

Polenta ai Funghi

Polenta with Mushrooms

Polenta was not originally made of corn, which did not appear in Italy until Christopher Columbus discovered South America, and was not much appreciated there until the 1700s. Before then *polenta* was made of chick-pea (garbanzo) flour, buckwheat, or other cereals. Ideally *polenta* is made in an unplated copper pot.

6 cups (48 fl oz/1.5 l) water
salt
2 cups (10 oz/300 g) coarse yellow cornmeal (maize flour)
10 oz (300 g) fresh *porcini, shiitake,* or cultivated (button) mushrooms
3 tablespoons extra-virgin olive oil
2 cloves garlic, thinly sliced
1 cup (8 fl oz/240 ml) heavy (double) cream
1 tablespoon chopped fresh flat-leaf (Italian) parsley

In a large saucepan over high heat, bring the water to a boil. Add a little salt and then pour in the cornmeal in a steady stream, while whisking continuously with a wire whisk. Reduce the heat to low and cook, stirring occasionally with a long wooden spoon, until the cornmeal is thick and pulls away from the sides of the pan, about 40 minutes.

Meanwhile, clean the mushrooms by rubbing them with a dry cloth or paper towel. If you are using *porcini*, use the mushrooms whole; if you are using *shiitake* or button mushrooms, discard the stems and slice the caps.

In a frying pan over low heat, warm the oil. Add the garlic and cook until translucent, about 2 minutes. Add the mushrooms and cook over medium heat until tender, about 5 minutes. Add the cream, bring to a boil, and sprinkle with the parsley and salt to taste.

Spoon the *polenta* onto a heated platter, cover with the cream-mushroom mixture, and serve immediately.

Serves 6

Polenta is becoming an important staple of the Italian table with its infinite variations. It is made from dent or flint corn, hard-kernel varieties. The soft-kernel varieties, arriving from the New World in little tin cans, are seen as a novelty. To produce more flavorful *polenta*, some small producers are reviving antique strains of corn that are considerably tastier than most modern hybrids. One such producer, Fattoria Scotti, insists on grinding the corn in an ancient water-driven stone mill that "cooks" the corn less than metal grinding plates do, and yields a pleasing, rough texture to the meal.

Ravioli ai Carciofi

Artichoke Ravioli

Ravioli, tortelli, and *agnolotti* are all the same thing. The names differ according to the region. In Lombardy, pasta filled with spinach and ricotta are known as *ravioli*; in Piedmont, pasta with the same filling are known as *agnolotti*; in Emilia-Romagna and Tuscany, they are known as *tortelli*.

½ cup (4 fl oz/120 ml) extra-virgin olive oil
10 oz (300 g) artichoke bottoms, trimmed and thinly sliced
1 clove garlic, minced
3 tablespoons freshly grated Parmesan cheese
1 tablespoon minced fresh mint, thyme, or flat-leaf (Italian) parsley
2⅓ cups (10 oz/300 g) all-purpose (plain) flour
3 extra-large eggs

In a large saucepan over low heat, warm 2 tablespoons of the oil. Add the artichoke bottoms and garlic, stir well, cover, and cook until tender, about 10 minutes. Turn out onto a cutting board and mince well. Transfer to a bowl, add the Parmesan and herb, and mix well. Set aside.

▓ Using the flour and eggs, make the pasta dough by following the step-by-step instructions on page 19.

▓ When the dough has been rolled out, cut it into strips about 4 in (10 cm) wide, then follow the step-by-step instructions for making *ravioli* on the facing page.

▓ Set the *ravioli* aside on a lightly floured surface or, if not cooking immediately, store covered with plastic wrap in the refrigerator for up to 6 hours.

▓ Bring a large saucepan of salted water to a boil. Reduce to a simmer and drop in the *ravioli*, a few at a time. As soon as they rise to the surface, in about 2 minutes, lift them out with a slotted spoon and place on a heated serving platter. When all the *ravioli* are cooked, pour the remaining oil over the top and serve immediately.

Serves 6

From top to bottom: Risotto with Quail, Artichoke Ravioli, Spinach Dumplings in Cabbage Sauce

1. Place tablespoon-sized mounds of the filling down the center of half of the dough strips, placing the mounds about 2 in (5 cm) apart. (Keep the rest of the dough strips covered.)

2. Using your finger or a pastry brush, paint water along the edges of the filled strips and the spaces between the mounds.

3. Cover each filled strip with a second strip of dough. Seal the two strips together around the sides and between the mounds of filling.

4. Using a fluted-edged cookie (biscuit) cutter about 2 in (5 cm) in diameter, cut out the mounds. Alternatively, cut into 2-in (5-cm) squares with a fluted-edged pastry wheel.

Gnocchetti alle Verze

Spinach Dumplings in Cabbage Sauce

10 oz (300 g) spinach, cooked, squeezed dry, and very finely chopped
2¾ cups (12 oz/360 g) all-purpose (plain) flour
1 tablespoon extra-virgin olive oil
2 eggs
salt and freshly ground pepper
¼ cup (2 oz/60 g) unsalted butter
1 onion, finely chopped
10 oz (300 g) Savoy cabbage leaves, shredded
½ cup (4 fl oz/120 ml) milk
½ cup (2 oz/60 g) freshly grated Parmesan cheese
½ cup (2 oz/60 g) freshly grated Fontina cheese

To make the *gnocchetti*, place the spinach in a mixing bowl. Add the flour, oil, and eggs. Season to taste with salt and pepper. Using your hands, knead the mixture until well amalgamated.

◼ Follow steps 2 and 3 of the step-by-step instructions for *gnocchi* on page 23, forming logs about 1 in (2.5 cm) in diameter and 4 in (10 cm) long and cutting them into ½-in (1.5-cm) lengths.

◼ To make the sauce, heat the butter in a large saucepan over medium heat. Add the onion and cook, stirring, until lightly golden, 8 to 10 minutes. Add the cabbage and season to taste with salt and pepper. Cook, uncovered, stirring frequently, for 10 minutes. Add the milk, reduce the heat to low; and cook gently for 20 minutes. Stir in both cheeses, remove the pan from the heat and set aside.

◼ To cook the *gnocchetti*, bring a large saucepan of salted water to a boil. Reduce the heat until the water is at a simmer and drop in the *gnocchetti*, a few at a time. As soon as they rise to the surface, after about 2 minutes, lift them out with a slotted spoon and add to the pan holding the cabbage sauce. When all the *gnocchetti* are in the sauce, cook over medium heat, stirring, for a few minutes. Arrange on a platter and serve immediately.

Serves 6

Risotto alle Quaglie

Risotto with Quail

6 quail
1 tablespoon chopped fresh rosemary
salt and freshly ground pepper
6 very thin slices *pancetta* or bacon
½ cup (4 oz/120 g) unsalted butter
1 bottle (3 cups/750 ml) Chianti Classico Riserva or other mature red wine
4 cups (32 fl oz/1 l) light meat stock
3 green (spring) onions, sliced
3¼ cups (1¼ lb/600 g) Arborio or Vialone nano rice
½ cup (2 oz/60 g) freshly grated Parmesan cheese

Preheat an oven to 325°F (165°C). Rub the quail with the rosemary and the salt and pepper to taste. Wrap each bird in a slice of *pancetta* and truss with kitchen string. Lay the birds in a roasting pan with 2 tablespoons of the butter.

Roast the quail in the preheated oven for about 30 minutes. As the birds cook, baste them with ½ cup (4 fl oz/120 ml) of the wine, adding a little at a time to keep them moist. Then cook the quail for another 30 minutes, during which time the *risotto* may be prepared.

To make the *risotto*, pour the stock into a saucepan and bring to a simmer over low heat. In a heavy saucepan over low heat, melt half of the remaining butter. Add the onions and cook until translucent, about 3 minutes. Add the rice, raise the heat to medium, and cook, stirring, for about 2 minutes. Add 1 cup of the simmering stock, and 1 cup of wine, and continue to stir. Continue adding stock and the remaining wine, a ladleful at a time, allowing most of the liquid to be absorbed before adding more liquid. Make sure that the rice is always covered with a thin layer of liquid.

Cook the rice for 15 minutes, counting from the first addition of stock, then remove the pan from the heat. Stir in the Parmesan and remaining butter. Season to taste with salt and pepper, cover, and set aside for 2 minutes to blend the flavors.

Spoon the *risotto* onto a heated serving platter, arrange the quail on top, and serve immediately.

Serves 6

I often serve a simple green salad at Coltibuono. It is perfect with roast chicken or after *risotto* with quail. The essential ingredients for a good salad are fresh greens and quality extra-virgin olive oil. I like to use a mixture of young leaves from various lettuces such as arugula, and fresh herbs, depending on the season and what is available in the garden. Wash and dry the leaves, then trim them. In a small cup, dissolve a pinch of salt in a tablespoon of red wine vinegar, and add ¼ cup of olive oil. Toss the salad with the dressing and season with freshly chopped herbs and ground pepper if desired.

I PIATTI DI MEZZO

Middle Courses

A *piatto di mezzo*, or "middle course," provides a brief pause between the two principal courses, the *primo piatto* and the *secondo piatto*. It is included in only the most elaborate and formal meals, served either at home or in an exclusive restaurant, and gives the guests an opportunity to relax for a moment and engage in conversation. It is also a convenient point at which to introduce the main wine of the meal, the vintage that would otherwise be poured with the *secondo piatto*.

Because a *piatto di mezzo* comes at a natural break in the flow of the meal, the dishes should be light and refreshing. They should cleanse the palate for the course and the wines that are to come. Pieces of crisp toasted bread topped with olive paste or slices of fresh mozzarella dressed with fruity olive oil and fresh basil leaves are particularly appropriate. So, too, are various egg dishes, such as *frittata arrotolata*, a thin omelet rolled around seasoned spinach; grilled polenta topped with delicately cooked eggs; or *sformatini di piselli in salsa di zucchine*, a savory custard mold laced with tender, green peas and covered with a silky sauce of zucchini and olive oil. Freshly baked flat breads, such as *piadina* or *schiacciata*, also make satisfying middle courses.

The vegetables that appear in such dishes should never also be included in courses that will come later in the meal. For example, if you serve *torta di spinaci*, savory pastry filled with spinach, pine nuts, and raisins, do not offer *spinaci agli amaretti* for the *contorno* or vegetable course. Or if you prepare *crostoni* with lettuce and *prosciutto*, do not also serve *involtini* made with lettuce wrappers.

A final rule to observe when preparing this course is to use fresh herbs whenever possible, preferably just picked from the garden. They will heighten the flavor of the other ingredients in the dish, resulting in the light, clean tastes ideally characteristic of every *piatto di mezzo*.

Crostoni di Lattuga al Prosciutto

Lettuce and Prosciutto on Toast

Crostoni are wonderful additions to a brunch or they may be served as a first course at an informal lunch. Other vegetables such as Swiss chard (silverbeet), halved fennel bulbs, or halved artichokes may be substituted for the lettuce.

6 small heads Boston (butterhead) lettuce
3 tablespoons unsalted butter
6 square slices white bread
6 thin slices Fontina or Swiss cheese, cut into the same size and shape as the bread
6 slices *prosciutto*
¾ cup (3 oz/90 g) freshly grated Parmesan cheese

Preheat an oven to 400°F (200°C). Cut out the hard stem from each lettuce head and then tie each head with kitchen string. Have a large bowl of ice water ready. Bring a large saucepan filled with salted water to a boil, add the heads, and boil for 1 minute. Drain and immerse in the ice water. Drain again and set aside on a cloth towel to dry.

▣ In a saucepan over low heat, melt 2 tablespoons of the butter. Add the lettuce heads and cook, turning gently, for about 3 minutes. Remove from the pan and snip and discard the strings. Butter the bread using the remaining 1 tablespoon butter. Toast the bread in the preheated oven until lightly browned, about 3 minutes. (The dish may be prepared ahead up to this point and assembled just before serving.)

▣ Top each toasted bread slice with a slice of cheese and a head of lettuce. Cover the lettuce with a slice of *prosciutto* and return the bread to the oven for about 5 minutes. Sprinkle the *crostoni* with Parmesan cheese and serve immediately.

Serves 6

Clockwise from top left: Salt Cod Salad with Red Beans, Grilled Polenta with Eggs, Lettuce and Prosciutto on Toast

Insalata di Baccalà e Fagioli

Salt Cod Salad with Red Beans

Salt cod is extremely popular all over Italy, but especially in the Veneto, Liguria, and Naples. The best *baccalà* is quite thick, about 1¼ in (3 cm) at its broadest point. When cod is noticeably yellow, it means that it is old and it should be passed up. It is most practical to buy filleted fish, even if one sacrifices a little flavor in doing so.

1¼ lb (600 g) filleted salt cod
1½ cups (10 oz/300 g) dried red kidney or pinto (*borlotti*) beans
⅓ cup (3 fl oz/90 ml) extra-virgin olive oil
juice of ½ lemon
salt and freshly ground pepper
6 fresh chives, chopped

To reconstitute the salt cod, put it in a bowl, add water to cover, and refrigerate for 24 hours, changing the water 4 times. It will be soft at this point. Drain and dry well with paper towels before using.

▩ Meanwhile, soak the beans in water to cover for about 12 hours. Drain, place in a large saucepan, and add water to cover by 1¼ in (3 cm). Cover and simmer over low heat until tender, about 1½ hours. Drain and set aside.

▩ To cook the cod, arrange it in a deep saucepan and cover generously with water. Bring the water to a boil, remove the pan from the heat, cover, and set aside until lukewarm. Drain the fish and arrange it in a salad bowl. Add the beans, oil, lemon juice, and salt and pepper to taste. Add the chives, mix gently, and serve.

Serves 6

Polenta alla Griglia

Grilled Polenta with Eggs

Polenta is a favorite dish in northern Italy. In the fall during truffle season, it is prepared with the richly flavored – quite costly – white truffle. Many northern Italians consider *polenta* prepared with grated truffle to be the best way to eat the highly prized fungus.

3 cups (24 fl oz/750 ml) water
salt
1 cup (5 oz/150 g) coarse yellow cornmeal (maize flour)
6 tablespoons (3 fl oz/90 ml) extra-virgin olive oil
6 eggs
salt and freshly ground pepper
⅓ cup (1½ oz/45 g) freshly grated Parmesan cheese

In a large saucepan over high heat, bring the water to a boil. Add a little salt and then pour in the cornmeal in a steady stream, while whisking continuously with a wire whisk. Reduce the heat to low and cook, stirring occasionally with a long wooden spoon, until the cornmeal is thick and pulls away from the sides of the pan, about 40 minutes.

▣ As soon as the *polenta* is cooked, rinse a 6-in (15-cm) square pan with cold water and pour the *polenta* into it. Press in well and let cool completely, then unmold and cut into 6 equal slices.

▣ Using 3 tablespoons of the oil, brush both sides of each slice with oil. Cook the slices on a hot grill, griddle or in a frying pan for about 3 minutes per side.

▣ Heat the remaining oil in a frying pan over medium heat. Break the eggs into the pan and fry until cooked to your liking. Season to taste with salt and pepper.

▣ Arrange the *polenta* slices on individual plates, place an egg on each slice, sprinkle with Parmesan cheese, and serve immediately.

Serves 6

One might say that *Parmigiano Reggiano* is the champagne of Parmesans. Like the wine, the cheese must come from a small, prescribed area near Parma and must conform to the strict rules of the local consortium if it is to be called a *Parmigiano Reggiano*. And also like the wine, it is a product of great quality and prestige. Each wheel of cheese begins its life as six hundred litres (150 gallons) of impeccably fresh milk. Cooked in huge copper vats, the curd is cut into rice-sized bits that give the cheese its grainy texture and its generic name, *grana*.

Caprese al Basilico
Mozzarella Salad with Oil and Basil

Caprese takes its name from its place of origin, Capri, where one can occasionally find pure buffalo mozzarella. The most commonly used mozzarella, however, is made from cow's milk and comes from the area around Sorrento. Buffalo's milk mozzarella is almost impossible to find nowadays, except in the spring in the region of Battipaglia or Caserta, near Naples. At other times of the year, this cheese is always made with part cow's milk, which lowers the quality.

1¼ lb (600 g) fresh mozzarella cheese
18 fresh basil leaves
freshly ground pepper
⅓ cup (3 fl oz/90 ml) extra-virgin olive oil

Cut the mozzarella into 18 slices. Arrange the slices, barely overlapping, on a dish. Place a basil leaf at each point where 2 slices meet. Season to taste with pepper, pour the oil over the cheese, and serve.

Serves 4 – 6

Clockwise from top left: Sausage and Cheese Wreath, Olive Bruschetta, Mozzarella Salad with Oil and Basil

Bruschetta alle Olive

Olive Bruschetta

Bruschetta, also called *fregolotta, fett'unta,* or *panunto,* depending upon the region, has spread from Italy throughout the world. It must be made with high-quality, extra-virgin olive oil. Tuscan oil, especially that from Chianti, is considered the best.

12 small black olives, pitted
6 capers, finely chopped
1 teaspoon fresh thyme leaves
2 tablespoons extra-virgin olive oil
salt and freshly ground pepper
2 slices coarse-textured bread

Preheat an oven to 350°F (180°C). Using a food processor fitted with the metal blade, mince the olives very finely. Stir in the capers, thyme, oil, and salt and pepper to taste.
▣ Toast the bread slices in the preheated oven until golden, about 5 minutes. While still hot, spread them with the olive paste and serve at once.

Serves 2

To be deemed extra-virgin olive oil, the oil must be taken from the first, cold pressing of the olives and must not contain more than 1 percent oleic acid. Color and flavor are also considered and, in the case of extra-virgin oil, both must be graded "perfect." Perfection comes in many flavors – extra-virgin oils are as varied as wines. Flavor and color are determined largely by the time of year when the olives are harvested. An early-harvest oil, from olives picked in November and December, is deep green with a pungent peppery bite; while a late harvest, between January and February, yields oil that is buttery and golden.

Ciambella alla Salsiccia e Formaggio

Sausage and Cheese Wreath

⅓ cup (3 fl oz/90 ml) lukewarm milk
⅓ cup (3 fl oz/90 ml) lukewarm water
2 cakes (½ oz/15 g *each*) fresh, compressed yeast or 2 packages
   (2½ teaspoons/¼ oz/7 g *each*) active dry yeast
2¾ cups (12 oz/360 g) all-purpose (plain) flour, plus flour for working
2 tablespoons unsalted butter, at room temperature
1 teaspoon sugar
1 teaspoon salt
5 oz (150 g) Neapolitan sausage or other spicy sausage, thickly sliced
5 oz (150 g) *provolone* cheese, roughly diced
1½ oz (45 g) *pancetta* or bacon, thickly sliced

In a small bowl combine the milk and water. Dissolve the yeast in liquid and set aside until foamy, about 10 minutes.

In a food processor fitted with the metal blade, combine the flour, butter, sugar, and salt and process for a couple of seconds. With the motor running pour in the yeast mixture and continue to process until the dough gathers in a rough ball around the blade. Remove to a lightly floured board and knead until smooth and elastic, about 5 minutes.

Shape the dough into a ball, place in a floured bowl, cover, and set aside in a warm place to rise until doubled, about 2 hours.

Meanwhile, make the filling. In a food processor fitted with the metal blade, roughly chop the sausage, *provolone*, and *pancetta*.

Turn the dough out onto a floured work surface, punch it down, and, with a rolling pin, flatten it out into a rectangle about 12 by 8 in (30 by 20 cm). Cover evenly with the sausage mixture, leaving the edges uncovered. Starting from one of the long sides, roll up the rectangle to enclose the filling. Bring the ends around to form a circle, then pinch the ends together securely.

Cover the wreath and let rise again in a warm place until doubled, about 1 hour. Meanwhile, preheat an oven to 400°F (200°C).

Bake in the preheated oven for 20 minutes. Reduce the heat to 350°F (180°C) and continue baking for 30 minutes. Remove from the oven and let cool before serving.

Serves 6

Frittata Arrotolata

Omelet Roll with Spinach

There are many variations on this recipe. Veal, turkey or chicken slices, ground (minced) meat, or even mashed potatoes can be used in place of the omelet. The filling can be made of a variety of vegetables, sausage, *mortadella*, smoked ham, *prosciutto*, or ground meat.

1 ¼ lb (600 g) spinach
3 tablespoons extra-virgin olive oil
pinch of freshly grated nutmeg
½ cup (2 oz/60 g) freshly grated Parmesan cheese
⅓ cup (2 oz/60 g) pine nuts, optional
6 extra-large eggs
salt and freshly ground pepper

Preheat an oven to 350°F (180°C).
▣ Bring a large saucepan of salted water to a boil, add the spinach, and boil for 1 minute. Drain well, squeeze dry, and chop.
▣ In a frying pan over low heat, warm 2 tablespoons of the oil. Add the spinach and cook, stirring, for about 3 minutes. Add the nutmeg and Parmesan cheese, stir well, and remove from the heat. Mix in the pine nuts and set aside.
▣ In a bowl beat the eggs with salt and pepper to taste. Heat the remaining 1 table-spoon oil in a large nonstick frying pan and cook the omelet, forming a roll as directed in the step-by-step instructions on the facing page.
▣ Place the *frittata* in the preheated oven until heated through, about 10 minutes. Cut into slices, arrange on a platter, and serve hot.

Serves 6

From top to bottom: Omelet Roll with Spinach, Deep-Fried Shrimp, Flat Bread Topped with Prosciutto

1. Heat the oil in a large non-stick frying pan over medium heat. Pour in the eggs and "poke" at them constantly with a wooden spoon until set.

2. Slide the omelet onto a work surface. Spread the spinach mixture over it in a layer about ⅜ in (1 cm) thick, leaving an uncovered ¾-in (2-cm) border around the entire edge. The border will keep the filling from leaking out when the omelet is rolled.

3. Roll up the omelet to enclose the spinach completely. Place seam-side down in an ovenproof dish and cook as directed.

Crocchette di Gamberoni

Deep-Fried Shrimp

This same batter may be used for frying pieces of salt cod, asparagus tips, sliced zucchini, or zucchini flowers. The frying must be done at the last minute so that the shrimp are still very hot and crunchy when served.

1¾ cups (7 oz/210 g) all-purpose (plain) flour
¼ cup (2 fl oz/60 ml) beer
3 eggs, separated
salt
5 cups (40 fl oz/1.2 l) extra-virgin olive oil or corn oil
18 large shrimp (prawns), peeled and deveined

In a bowl mix the flour and beer to make a thick, smooth batter. Add the egg yolks, one at a time, and then salt to taste.

▣ In a separate bowl beat the egg whites to form soft peaks and gently fold them into the batter. Let stand for 30 minutes.

▣ In a deep saucepan heat the oil to 340°F (170°C). Dip the shrimp, one at a time, into the batter to coat well. Drop them, a few at a time, into the hot oil; do not crowd the pan. Fry until deep golden, about 3 minutes. Turn them over and fry on the other side for 2 more minutes. Lift out with a slotted spoon, drain on paper towels, and arrange on a heated platter. Repeat with the remaining shrimp. Serve very hot.

Serves 6

Piadina al Prosciutto

Flat Bread Topped with Prosciutto

Piadina is the Emilia-Romagna version of Tuscan *schiacciata* and Ligurian *focaccia*. The recipe is classically made from flour, lard, and water, but here it has been refined to produce a lighter bread. And in the absence of the traditional metal plates and grill – *testaroh* – used for cooking *piadina*, I have found that nonstick pans work very well.

2⅓ cups (10 oz/300 g) all-purpose (plain) flour, plus flour for working
⅔ cup (5 fl oz/150 ml) milk
¼ cup (2 oz/60 g) unsalted butter
1 teaspoon baking powder
salt
6 slices *prosciutto*

In a food processor fitted with the plastic blade, combine the flour, milk, butter, baking powder, and a pinch of salt. Process until a soft dough forms, a couple of minutes.

▨ On a lightly floured board knead the dough for a couple of minutes until smooth, then shape into a ball and place in a floured bowl. Cover with a towel and let rest for 30 minutes.

▨ Divide the dough into 6 equal pieces. On a lightly floured board, roll out each piece into a disk about 5 in (12 cm) in diameter and about ⅛ in (2 mm) thick.

▨ Heat a nonstick frying pan over medium heat. When it begins to smoke, slip in a disk and cook for about 3 minutes. Using a spatula, flip it over, place a light plate on top as a weight, and cook for about 2 minutes.

▨ Remove from the pan and repeat with the remaining disks. Let the *piadine* cool slightly, then top each with a slice of *prosciutto*.

Serves 6

Parma is home to some of Italy's finest *prosciutto*. The hams begin as sleek hogs fattened on grain, acorns, and whey left over from the making of Parmesan cheese. This clever recycling makes for succulent flesh, which is left sweet by a modest use of salt. Most hams are heavily salted to prevent their spoiling, but the air of the Langhirano Valley is dry enough to prevent it naturally. After an initial salting, the hams are taken through a long *prosciugamento* (drying process). They hang by the thousands in large wooden warehouses with louvered walls that allow breezes to circulate inside, drying the meat.

Pomodori Ripieni

Stuffed Tomatoes

Tomatoes can be stuffed with many different fillings, including chopped mozzarella, canned tuna, beans and onions, or ricotta mixed with herbs. These tomatoes are perfect for a first course. They can be stuffed up to six hours in advance of serving and refrigerated. Bring to room temperature before serving.

1 cup (6 oz/180 g) dried white beans
6 large tomatoes
salt
½ red (Spanish) onion, sliced paper-thin
2 tablespoons minced fresh flat-leaf (Italian) parsley
½ cup (4 oz/120 g) canned tuna, drained and flaked
½ cup (4 fl oz/120 ml) extra-virgin olive oil
freshly ground pepper

Soak the beans in water to cover for about 12 hours. Drain and place in a saucepan. Add water to cover by 1¼ in (3 cm), cover, and simmer over low heat until tender, about 1½ hours. Drain and let cool.

▣ Slice off the tops of the tomatoes. Using a spoon scoop out the seeds and most of the flesh. Lightly salt the inside of each tomato and then invert to drain for about 30 minutes.

▣ In a bowl stir together the beans, onion, parsley, tuna, and oil. Season to taste with salt and pepper. Spoon the bean mixture into the tomatoes, arrange on a platter, and serve.

Serves 6

Sformatini di Piselli in Salsa di Zucchine

Green Pea Timbale in Zucchini Sauce

In the past vegetable molds were often eaten at family meals, after the soup. Now they are served only as a *piatto di mezzo* for a formal dinner party.

3 tablespoons unsalted butter
¼ cup (1 oz/30 g) all-purpose (plain) flour
1 cup (8 fl oz/240 ml) milk
2 large eggs, beaten
2 ¼ cups (1¼ lb/600 g) shelled green peas, blanched for 2 minutes
½ cup (2 oz/60 g) fine, dry bread crumbs
1¼ lb (600 g) zucchini (courgettes), blanched for 3 minutes
⅓ cup (3 fl oz/90 ml) extra-virgin olive oil

Preheat an oven to 350°F (180°C). In a saucepan over medium heat, melt 2 tablespoons of the butter. Stir in the flour and cook, stirring, for a couple of minutes until absorbed. Add the milk, a little at a time, and cook, stirring, until a fairly thick sauce forms, about 5 minutes. Remove from the heat and let cool.

▨ Add the eggs and peas to the sauce, mixing gently. Rub six 1-cup (8-fl oz/240-ml) molds with the remaining 1 tablespoon butter and then coat with the bread crumbs. Divide the pea mixture evenly among the molds. Place molds in a baking dish and pour in hot water to reach halfway up their sides. Bake in the preheated oven until a toothpick inserted in the center comes out dry, about 30 minutes.

▨ Meanwhile, to make the sauce, use a vegetable peeler to remove the green skins from the zucchini; set aside the flesh for another use. In a food processor fitted with a metal blade, combine the skins and oil and purée. Transfer to a saucepan, add 3 tablespoons of water, cover, and cook over low heat for about 2 minutes.

▨ To serve, run a knife blade around the edge of each mold and invert onto a heated platter. Pour the sauce over them and serve immediately.

Serves 6

From top to bottom: Ham Mousse with Melon Sauce, Green Pea Timbale in Zucchini Sauce

Sformato di Prosciutto

Ham Mousse with Melon Sauce

To judge whether a melon is ripe, press the end opposite the stem end with your thumb. The rind should yield but still be elastic. If it is too soft, the melon is overripe; if it is too hard, the melon will be bitter. A second test is to smell the melon. It will have a pleasant ripe fragrance if it is ready to eat.

10 oz (300 g) thinly sliced ham
2 cups (1 lb/450 g) ricotta
⅓ cup (3 fl oz/90 ml) Vin Santo, Port, or Madeira
2 envelopes (½ oz/15 g) unflavored powdered gelatin
1 large cantaloupe

In a food processor fitted with the metal blade, finely chop the ham. Add the ricotta and process until smooth.

▣ In a small pan heat the wine gently, remove from the heat, and sprinkle the gelatin on top. Stir until the gelatin melts, then add to the ham-ricotta mixture in the processor. Pulse a few times just to mix.

▣ Rinse a 4-cup (32-fl oz/1-l) mold with cold water and fill it with the ham mixture. Cover and refrigerate for about 5 hours or for up to 12 hours.

▣ Peel the melon, remove and discard the seeds and fibers, and cut into chunks. Put the melon in a food processor fitted with the metal blade and process until creamy.

▣ To unmold the mousse, dip the base of the mold into a pan of boiling water for 5 seconds. Invert a plate on top of the mold, hold it firmly in place, and invert the mold. If the mousse sticks, repeat the steps. Pour the melon sauce around the mousse and serve.

Serves 6

Schiacciata di Formaggio

Flat Bread with Cheese

2 cakes (½ oz/15 g *each*) fresh, compressed yeast or 2 packages
   (2½ teaspoons/¼ oz/7 g *each*) active dry yeast
¾ cup plus 2 tablespoons (7 fl oz/210 ml) lukewarm water
2¾ cups (12 oz/360 g) all-purpose (plain) flour, plus flour for working
¼ cup (2 fl oz/60 ml) extra-virgin olive oil
big pinch of coarse salt
2 oz (60 g) Fontina or Swiss cheese, sliced
2 oz (60 g) soft, ripe cheese such as *taleggio* or Gorgonzola

In a small bowl dissolve the yeast in the water and set aside until foamy, about 10 minutes.
▨ Heap the flour in a mound in a large bowl. Make a well in the center and gradually add
the yeast mixture, stirring in a circular motion with a fork until a dough forms.
▨ Turn the dough out onto a lightly floured work surface and knead until smooth and
elastic, about 10 minutes. Shape the dough into a ball, put in an oiled bowl, cover, and set
aside in a warm place to rise until doubled, about 2 hours.
▨ Brush a 10-in (25-cm) tart pan with some of the oil. On a lightly floured surface,
punch down the dough and roll it out into a round the same size as the pan. Transfer the
round to the pan, cover, and let rise again until doubled in thickness, about 20 minutes.
▨ Preheat an oven to 400°F (200°C). Brush the *schiacciata* with the remaining oil,
sprinkle with the salt, and bake it in the preheated oven until lightly golden, about 30
minutes.
▨ Let the bread cool a little and then cut in half horizontally. Layer the 2 cheeses on the
bottom half, replace the top half, and cut into wedges to serve.

Serves 6

Carpaccio al Balsamico

Carpaccio with Balsamic Vinegar

Known from ancient times, balsamic vinegar is now produced commercially in Modena and Reggio Emilia. It is especially delicious with raw tomatoes, because its sweetness counterbalances the natural acidity of the tomatoes. *Carpaccio* in Italian refers to raw meat that is sliced or chopped and served with a condiment.

10 oz (300 g) lean beef, ground (minced) twice
2 tablespoons mixed, finely minced fresh herbs such as flat-leaf (Italian)
   parsley, basil, thyme, and chives
salt and freshly ground pepper
2 tablespoons balsamic vinegar
2 tablespoons extra-virgin olive oil

Combine the meat with the herbs and salt and pepper to taste and mix well. Form the mixture into 2 balls and flatten each onto a separate plate. Make a well in the middle of each patty. (At this point the patties may be covered with plastic wrap and refrigerated for up to 2 hours. Remove from the refrigerator just before serving.)

▨ In a small bowl whisk together the vinegar, oil, and salt and pepper to taste.
▨ Divide the vinegar mixture evenly between the wells and serve immediately.

Serves 2

From top to bottom: Flat Bread with Cheese, Carpaccio with Balsamic Vinegar

The use of balsamic vinegar or *balsamico* was once a sign of nobility. The presence of this condiment in noble houses indicated that the family had land for growing grapes, space for the ranks of aging barrels, and people with time to tend the *balsamico*. In order for it to carry the coveted title *Tradizionale, balsamico* must age for a minimum of twelve years, and some are aged for as much as a century. *Balsamico* does not begin as wine, but rather as the juice of selected grapes, which is boiled to concentrate the sugar. This dark, tart-sweet syrup, called *saba,* is barrel-aged in various hardwoods.

Torta di Spinaci

Spinach Tart

2 cups (8 oz/240 g) all-purpose (plain) flour, plus flour for working
salt
½ cup (4 oz/120 g) unsalted butter, cut into small pieces, plus 1 tablespoon extra for pan
1 egg yolk plus 3 whole eggs, beaten
3 tablespoons milk
10 oz (300 g) spinach, blanched 1 minute, drained and squeezed dry, and chopped
¼ cup (1 oz/30 g) golden raisins, soaked in water to cover for 30 minutes and drained
¾ cup (6 fl oz/180 ml) heavy (double) cream
½ cup (2 oz/ 60 g) freshly grated Parmesan cheese
salt and freshly ground pepper
2½ tablespoons (1 oz/30 g) pine nuts

To make the dough by hand, pour the flour into a bowl and add the salt and the ½ cup
(4 oz/120 g) butter. Using your fingertips work the butter into the flour until a crumbly
dough forms. Add the egg yolk and milk, incorporate thoroughly, and knead the dough into
a ball. Wrap the ball in plastic wrap and refrigerate for 1 hour.
▧ To make the dough in a food processor, combine the flour and salt in the work bowl
fitted with the metal blade. Process briefly to mix. Add the ½ cup (4 oz/120 g) butter and
process until the ingredients resemble coarse meal. Add the egg yolk and milk and process
until the dough forms a ball around the blade. Wrap the dough in plastic and refrigerate for
1 hour.
▧ Preheat an oven to 350°F (180°C).
▧ Using 1 tablespoon butter, grease a 9-in (23-cm) tart pan with removable bottom and
then dust it lightly with flour. On a lightly floured work surface, roll out the dough into a
round about 1 in (2.5 cm) larger in diameter than the pan. Line the prepared pan with the
pastry and trim off the top even with the rim.
▧ In a bowl combine the spinach, raisins, whole eggs, cream, and Parmesan. Mix well and
season with salt and pepper to taste. Pour into the pastry-lined pan. Top with the pine nuts.
▧ Bake in the preheated oven until golden, about 40 minutes. Let cool slightly then
transfer to a dish. Serve lukewarm or cool.

Serves 6

I SECONDI

Main Courses

The *secondo piatto*, or main course of a meal, generally consists of fish, shellfish, meat, or fowl. It could be a very plain grilled chop or a more intricate sauce-bathed whole fish. In either case the course usually comes unadorned or with the vegetable course arranged around the serving platter.

Italy is blessed with long coastlines, so fish and shellfish are popular main courses. Some restaurants even keep their own fishing boats, offering whatever is caught that day as the special *secondo piatto*. *Trance di branzino ai carciofi*, sea bass with artichokes, and *filetti di sogliola alle olive*, sole fillets with sharp-flavored olives, are two of the infinite possibilities.

Many different kinds of fowl have traditionally appeared as *secondi piatti* on the Italian table, from the prosaic chicken to a variety of small birds. In the old stone houses of Tuscany and Umbria, one can still see tiny holes where wild birds nested, only to be plucked from their homes by the *contadini* for roasting over an open fire. In the Veneto the castles and houses of the Middle Ages were equipped with dovecotes that ensured a steady supply of squabs for the residents. Because these small birds are such prolific breeders, only a few pairs were necessary to fulfill a family's needs. Then, as now, squabs were slaughtered when young, before they learned to fly, so that the meat was particularly tender and delicate.

Rabbit is also prized for its delicacy. It, too, is best when eaten young, at six months or less, and many people have found it easy to raise a few rabbits for the table. At one time rabbits were bred in great numbers in cages for the restaurant at Badia a Coltibuono. But the father of the rabbit keeper discovered that his son was not cleaning the cages properly and, in a fit of temper, broke them open and freed the rabbits. Today the descendants of the original restaurant stock run rampant in the surrounding fields and woods.

Regardless of which dish you serve for the *secondo piatto*, it is critical that it be set out on the table at the proper temperature. Each of the recipes that follows indicates the optimal temperature. The fine subtleties of a dish are lost when it is served too hot or too cold, and the success of the entire meal is compromised.

Stinco di Vitello al Sedano

Veal Shank in Celery Sauce

Veal shank is the entire hock of veal, the same part that, sliced, is used for *ossibuchi*.
To be tender, it must be cooked a very long time. You can substitute fennel or artichokes for
the celery in the accompanying sauce.

3 tablespoons all-purpose (plain) flour
salt and freshly ground pepper
2 veal shanks, about 2½ lb (1.2 kg) each
3 tablespoons extra-virgin olive oil
12 stalks celery, preferably white, peeled and cut into pieces
1 cup (8 fl oz/240 ml) milk
1 cup (8 fl oz/240 ml) dry white wine, plus extra if needed

Preheat an oven to 325°F (160°C).

▨ In a bowl mix together the flour with salt to taste. Dredge the shanks in the flour mixture. Heat the oil in a roasting pan over medium heat. Add the shanks to the pan and
brown on all sides, about 10 minutes. Add the celery and place in the preheated oven until
very tender, about 4 hours.

▨ After the first 2 hours, pour in the milk. When that cooks away, add the white wine, a
little at a time.

▨ Arrange the cooked shanks on a heated platter and keep warm.

▨ Using a hand blender, purée the celery with the cooking juices, or pass through a food
mill. Pour the sauce into the roasting pan and place over medium heat, adding additional
wine if too dry. Pour into a bowl and serve immediately alongside the shanks.

Serves 6

From top to bottom: Squab with Juniper Berries, Veal Shank in Celery Sauce, Chicken Roasted with Herbs

Pollo Arrosto alle Erbe

Chicken Roasted with Herbs

This is a specialty throughout Italy and the world. The only times I have eaten it cooked to perfection – with crunchy golden skin and tender meat – have been when it was made by Romola, the cook at Coltibuono for twenty-six years, or by Maro Spender Gorky, an English friend who has lived in Chianti for thirty years. The crunchy skin is the result of cooking the chicken in plenty of oil (which you later remove) and using an aluminum roasting pan.

1 tablespoon fresh thyme leaves
1 tablespoon fresh oregano leaves, finely chopped
1 tablespoon fresh rosemary leaves, finely chopped
1 tablespoon fresh sage leaves, finely chopped
1 tablespoon grated lemon zest
salt and freshly ground pepper
1 roasting chicken, about 4 lb (1.8 kg)
⅓ cup (3 fl oz/90 ml) extra-virgin olive oil
½ cup (4 fl oz/120 ml) dry white wine

Preheat an oven to 325°F (160°C). In a small bowl mix together the herbs, lemon zest, and salt and pepper to taste. Using your fingers lift and separate the chicken skin from the meat and insert the mixture in between to cover the breast completely. Truss the bird with kitchen string.

◼ Pour the oil into a roasting pan and place the chicken in it. Cook in the preheated oven for about 2 hours, turning occasionally and basting with the cooking juices. Raise the heat to 375°F (190°C) and cook until the chicken becomes quite dark, about 30 minutes.

◼ Remove the chicken from the oven and snip and remove the string. Place the bird on a heated platter and keep warm.

◼ Pour the fat off the pan juices. Heat the juices over medium heat, add the wine, and deglaze the pan. Pour into a bowl and serve immediately alongside the chicken.

Serves 6

Piccioni al Ginepro

Squab with Juniper Berries

Squab may be stuffed and roasted, stewed, or cooked on a spit. They are often served with *polenta* or *risotto*. The squab should cook for about 1½ hours so that the skin turns golden and the meat is easily removed from the bone.

3 slices coarse-textured bread
1 cup (8 fl oz/240 ml) milk
1 egg
½ cup (2 oz/60 g) freshly grated Parmesan cheese
2 oz (60 g) ham, finely chopped
2 tablespoons minced juniper berries
salt and freshly ground pepper
3 squab (pigeons) or Cornish hens, about 1¼ lb (600 g) each
2 tablespoons unsalted butter
2 tablespoons extra-virgin olive oil
¾ cup (6 fl oz/180 ml) red wine

Preheat an oven to 325°F (160°C). In a bowl soak the bread in the milk for about 10 minutes. Drain and squeeze dry. In a mixing bowl combine the bread, egg, Parmesan, ham, and juniper berries. Season to taste with salt and pepper. Stuff the squab with this mixture, truss with kitchen string, and arrange in a roasting pan with the butter and oil. Bake in the preheated oven for about 1 hour.

▨ Using half of the wine, pour it into the pan in small amounts at regular intervals while continuing to cook the squab until tender, another 30 minutes.

▨ Remove the squab from the oven and snip and remove the strings. Cut in half lengthwise and place on a heated platter; keep warm.

▨ Heat the cooking juices over medium heat. Add the remaining wine and deglaze the pan. Pour through a strainer over the squab and serve immediately.

Serves 6

Scampi all'Arancia

Scampi in Orange Sauce

6 lb (3 kg) whole scampi or whole large prawns in the shell or 2½ lb (1.2 kg) peeled
¾ cup (6 oz/180 g) orange marmalade
⅓ cup (3 fl oz/90 ml) sweet dessert wine
¼ cup (2 oz/60 g) unsalted butter
salt and freshly ground pepper

If using whole scampi or prawns, remove and discard the heads and shells. Devein. Set aside.
In a saucepan combine the marmalade and wine and cook over low heat for about 5 minutes. In a large frying pan over medium heat, melt the butter. Add the shrimp and sauté for 2 minutes. Season to taste with salt and pepper. Pour in the marmalade sauce and cook for 1 minute. Arrange the scampi on a heated platter and serve immediately.

Pesce alle Erbe

Whole Fish with Herbs

2 tablespoons extra-virgin olive oil
2 or 3 lemons, sliced
1 whole red snapper (sea bream or porgie), about 4 lb (2 kg)
salt and freshly ground pepper
1 tablespoon each of fresh thyme leaves, fresh oregano leaves, fresh chives, fresh
   fennel sprigs, all finely chopped
1 tablespoon grated lemon zest
⅓ cup (3 fl oz/90 ml) dry white wine

Preheat an oven to 350°F (180°C). Combine the oil and lemon slices in a shallow roasting pan, spreading the slices out to cover the bottom of the pan. Season the clean fish inside and out with salt and pepper. Sprinkle the herbs and lemon zest over the fish and in the cavity. Lay the fish in the pan. Add the wine.
Bake the fish for 30 minutes, turning it once and basting occasionally. Arrange the fish on a platter, discarding the lemon. Serve at once.

Both recipes serve 6

Costolette di Tonno al Vino Rosso

Fresh Tuna in Red Wine

Tuna is caught mainly in the spring, when it leaves the deep water and comes closer to the coast. Although some people believe that only white wine should be used with seafood, low-tannin red wines are perfect with tuna, swordfish, cod, prawns, and lobster.

6 tuna steaks about 7 oz (210 g) each
⅓ cup (3 oz/90 g) all-purpose (plain) flour
3 tablespoons extra-virgin olive oil
6 tablespoons (3 oz/90 g) green peppercorns, crushed with a knife blade
3 bay leaves
1 cup (8 fl oz/240 ml) good-quality, light red wine
salt

Dredge the tuna lightly in the flour, shaking off any excess.
▣ In a large frying pan over medium heat, warm the oil. Add the tuna and cook for 3 minutes on each side. Add the peppercorns, bay leaves, and wine. Season to taste with salt. Lower the heat, cover, and cook for 5 minutes, turning once.
▣ Arrange the tuna on a heated platter. Remove and discard the bay leaves, pour on the sauce, and serve immediately.

Serves 6

From top to bottom: Fillets of Sole with Black Olives, Shrimp in Orange Sauce, Fresh Tuna in Red Wine

Filetti di Sogliola alle Olive
Fillets of Sole with Black Olives

Black or green olives can be used for this dish. Green olives are harvested at the end of summer, before they are fully mature, and the black ones are harvested after Christmas. The largest olives come from Bari in southern Italy. Those from Gaeta, in Lazio, are smaller and more suitable for cooking. Green olives, being larger and more acidic, are better for serving with apéritifs.

2 tomatoes, peeled
salt
3 tablespoons extra-virgin olive oil
6 sole fillets, about 7 oz (210 g) each
¼ cup (2 fl oz/60 ml) dry white wine
18 Gaeta olives or other mild, black olives in brine
2 tablespoons balsamic vinegar
1 handful of fresh basil leaves, shredded

Cut the tomatoes in half, remove and discard the seeds, and dice into cubes. Place in a colander, sprinkle with salt, and let drain for about 30 minutes.

◼ In a frying pan over medium heat, warm the oil. Add the sole and cook for 2 minutes on each side. Add the wine, olives, and salt to taste. Reduce the heat to low and cook for 3 minutes, gently turning once. Add the vinegar and tomato and sprinkle with the basil. Cover, remove from the heat, and let stand for 1 minute to allow the flavors to blend.

◼ Arrange the sole on a heated platter, pour on the sauce, and serve immediately.

Serves 6

Polpettone alle Uova Sode

Meatroll with Eggs

½ cup (2 oz/60 g) bread crumbs from coarse-textured bread
1 cup (8 fl oz/240 ml) milk
1¼ lb (600 g) ground (minced) lean beef
10 oz (300 g) *mortadella*, ground
2 raw eggs, plus 4 hard-cooked eggs, shelled
pinch of freshly grated nutmeg
1 tablespoon minced fresh rosemary
salt and freshly ground pepper
1 tablespoon unsalted butter
2 tablespoons extra-virgin olive oil
1 cup (8 fl oz/240 ml) dry white wine

Preheat an oven to 350° (180°). In a bowl, soak the bread crumbs in the milk for about 10 minutes. Drain and squeeze dry.

In a mixing bowl, combine the bread crumbs, beef, *mortadella*, the 2 raw eggs, nutmeg, rosemary, and salt and pepper to taste. Mix all ingredients until they form a pastelike consistency.

On your work surface, flatten the mixture using the palms of your hands to form a rectangle about 9 in (23 cm) long , 6 in (15 cm) wide, and ⅜ in (1 cm) thick. Cut a thin slice off the ends of each hard-cooked egg to form flat surfaces and place the eggs end to end in a row running lengthwise down the center of the rectangle. Wrap the meat over the eggs, forming a large sausage, patting the ends together to seal them.

Melt the butter with the oil in a roasting pan and then place the meatroll in the pan. Bake in a preheated oven, turning once using a spatula, until golden brown, about 1½ hours. Using ½ cup (4 fl oz/120 ml) of the wine, baste the meatroll several times during the cooking.

Remove the meatroll from the pan and keep warm. Place the pan over medium heat, add the remaining ½ cup (4 fl oz/120 ml) wine, and deglaze the pan juices. Slice the meatroll, arrange the slices on a serving dish, pour the pan juices over them and serve piping hot. This is also excellent when served cold the following day.

Serves 6

Trance di Branzino ai Carciofi

Sea Bass with Sautéed Artichokes

Sea bass, also known in Italy as *spigola*, has firm, flavorful meat that may be cooked in many ways. Tuna, swordfish, or cod may be prepared in this manner, and the artichokes can be replaced with fennel or, for a more refined dish, such mushrooms as *porcini*, morels, or *shiitake*. If fresh marjoram is unavailable, use oregano, basil, or mint.

6 small or 3 large artichokes
juice of 1 lemon, plus 2 lemons, thinly sliced
⅓ cup (3 fl oz/90 ml) extra-virgin olive oil
6 sea bass steaks, about 8 oz (240 g) each
salt and freshly ground pepper
⅓ cup (3 fl oz/90 ml) dry white wine
2 tablespoons fresh marjoram leaves

Preheat an oven to 400°F (200°C). Fill a large bowl with cold water and add the lemon juice. Trim the artichokes by removing the stems, tough outer leaves, and chokes. Slice thinly lengthwise and transfer to the bowl, to prevent them from discoloring.

▣ Pour 2 tablespoons of the oil into a roasting pan. Arrange half of the lemon slices in the pan and place the fish on them. Season to taste with salt and pepper and cover with the remaining lemon slices. Pour in 2 more tablespoons of oil and the wine. Place in the preheated oven and cook for about 10 minutes.

▣ Meanwhile, heat the remaining 2 tablespoons of oil in a frying pan over low heat. Add the artichokes, season to taste with salt and pepper, cover, and cook, stirring occasionally, until tender, about 10 minutes.

▣ Remove the fish from the oven, discard the lemon slices, and arrange on a heated platter. Scatter the artichokes over the top, sprinkle with the marjoram, and serve immediately.

Serves 6

From top to bottom: Meatroll with Eggs, Sea Bass with Sautéed Artichokes

Filetti di Trota in Salsa di Finocchio

Trout Fillets in Fennel Sauce

This sauce is delicious, not only on trout fillets, but also on other fish or on spaghetti, boiled rice, or even vegetables. Green (spring) onions or globe onions can be substituted for the leeks, and carrots or broccoli can be used in place of the fennel.

2 leeks
2 fennel bulbs, trimmed and thinly sliced crosswise
½ cup (4 fl oz/120 ml) extra-virgin olive oil
½ cup (4 fl oz/120 ml) dry white wine
12 trout fillets
salt and freshly ground pepper

Cut off and discard the green parts of the leeks. Cut in half lengthwise, gently open the leaves, and rinse under cold water. Bring a saucepan filled with water to a boil, add the leeks, and blanch for 2 minutes. Drain and slice thinly.

▣ In a saucepan over low heat, combine the leeks, fennel, 2 tablespoons of the oil, and half the wine. Cover and cook, stirring occasionally, until tender, about 10 minutes.

▣ Using a hand blender, purée the leek mixture. Add 2 tablespoons of the oil and blend briefly. Return the sauce to low heat and cook until reduced by half. Season to taste with salt and pepper.

▣ Meanwhile, put the trout fillets in a large frying pan, pour on the remaining oil, season to taste with salt and pepper, and add the remaining wine. Cover and cook over low heat about 5 minutes, turning once very gently.

▣ Arrange the trout on a heated platter, pour on the hot sauce, and serve immediately.

Serves 6

Petti di Pollo in Salsa di Fegatini

Chicken Breast in Liver Sauce

Italians use chicken livers for making pâtés, *crostini* (especially in Tuscany), and sauces, or they sauté them with butter and sage. They turn up as the principal ingredient in a rice timbale, in pastas, and in many *ravioli* fillings. Chicken livers should be cleaned well before cooking. Any fat should be removed and the gall bladder, which is very bitter, discarded. The freshest livers are almost pink. If they are dark, they are too old.

¼ oz (6 g) dried *porcini* or fresh *shiitake* or cultivated (button) mushrooms
⅓ cup (3 fl oz/90 ml) extra-virgin olive oil
1 clove garlic, minced
3 chicken livers, cleaned
6 fresh sage leaves
1 anchovy fillet in oil, drained
1 tablespoon capers, drained
1 cup (8 fl oz/240 ml) semisweet white wine
3 whole chicken breasts, skinned, cleaned, and cut in half lengthwise
salt and freshly ground pepper

If using *porcini*, soak in water to cover for about 30 minutes. Drain and squeeze dry.

▦ To make the sauce, heat 3 tablespoons of the oil in a saucepan over medium heat. Add the garlic, livers, and sage and cook over medium heat, stirring occasionally, for about 5 minutes. Add the mushrooms, anchovy, capers, and wine. Cover and cook over low heat for 5 minutes. Remove from the heat and purée with a hand blender.

▦ In a frying pan over medium heat, warm the remaining oil. Add the chicken breasts and cook, turning occasionally, for about 10 minutes. Reduce the heat, pour the liver sauce into the pan (it should cover the chicken), cover, and cook for 5 minutes, adding water if necessary to keep the dish very moist. Season to taste with salt and pepper and serve immediately.

Serves 6

Clockwise from top right: Chicken Breast in Liver Sauce, Ossibuchi with Lemon and Parsley, Rabbit in Caper Sauce with Basil

Ossibuchi in Gremolata

Ossibuchi with Lemon and Parsley

Ossibuchi are wide slices of the hock on the front or rear leg of veal. The best quality is from the center portion of the rear leg, as those slices have more marrow. Of the numerous recipes for *ossibuchi*, many of which require tomatoes, this one, with its simple garnish of lemon zest and chopped parsley, is the most delicate. Traditionally *ossibuchi* are served with *risotto* finished with freshly grated Parmesan cheese or, in the Milanese style, tinted with saffron. They are also excellent with peas or mashed potatoes.

6 *ossibuchi*, about 10 oz (300 g) each
⅓ cup (1½ oz/45 g) all-purpose (plain) flour
¼ cup (2 oz/60 g) unsalted butter
1 small onion, thinly sliced
salt
2 cups (450 ml) dry white wine
grated zest of 1 lemon
3 tablespoons minced fresh flat-leaf (Italian) parsley

Pierce the skin surrounding the *ossibuchi* so that they do not curl when cooked. Tie a length of kitchen string around each slice. Dredge lightly in the flour, shaking off any excess.

▣ In a frying pan over low heat, melt the butter. Add the onion and cook until translucent, about 3 minutes. Add the *ossibuchi*, increase the heat to medium, and cook until they begin to color, about 5 minutes on each side. Season to taste with salt, pour in half of the wine, cover, and cook over low heat until very tender, about 2 hours. During this time add the remaining wine, a little at a time, so that the pan is always moist. If necessary, add water in small amounts.

▣ Sprinkle with the lemon zest and parsley and check for seasoning. Arrange on a heated platter and serve immediately.

Serves 6

Coniglio ai Capperi e Basilico

Rabbit in Caper Sauce with Basil

Rabbit is popular in Italy, where it is usually butchered young, at six months or less. It is often cooked in a wine marinade or roasted *alla cacciatora*, with tomato and mushrooms. For the most elegant preparation, only the saddle is used. The following recipe can also be used for chicken or veal.

1 tablespoon extra-virgin olive oil
1 rabbit, about 4 lb (1.8 kg), cut into serving pieces
2 tablespoons all-purpose (plain) flour
1 carrot, cut into pieces
1 onion, cut into pieces
1 stalk celery, cut into pieces
6 fresh plum (egg) tomatoes, peeled, or canned with their liquid
1 handful of fresh flat-leaf (Italian) parsley, chopped
6 fresh chives, chopped
1 cup (8 fl oz/240 ml) dry white wine
salt and freshly ground pepper
3 tablespoons capers, well drained
1 handful of fresh basil leaves, torn into pieces

Heat the oil in a heavy pan over medium heat. Add the rabbit pieces and cook until golden brown on all sides, about 10 minutes. Sprinkle with the flour and add the vegetables, parsley, and chives. Pour in the wine, season to taste with the salt and pepper, cover, and cook over low heat about 1½ hours, adding a little water if necessary to keep the rabbit moist.

▣ Remove the rabbit to a heated serving dish and keep hot.

▣ Purée the juices and vegetables with a hand blender. Reheat the purée and stir in the capers. Pour over the rabbit, sprinkle with the basil, and serve immediately.

Serves 6

Clockwise from top left: Pork Chops with Prunes, Lamb Fricassée with Fresh Tarragon, Beef Braised in Red Wine with Cloves

Manzo ai Chiodi di Garofano

Beef Braised in Red Wine with Cloves

Whether known as *brasato, stufato,* or *stracotto,* this dish of many names varies not only from region to region but also within them. It is, however, always based on a wine marinade and flavored with vegetables and spices or herbs.

18 whole cloves
2½ lb (1.2 kg) beef suited for braising, in one piece
1 bottle (25 fl oz/750 ml) good-quality, aged red wine
2 onions, cut into pieces
4 stalks celery, cut into pieces
4 carrots, cut into pieces
2 tablespoons extra-virgin olive oil
1 tablespoon unsalted butter
salt

Stick the cloves into the meat and place in a large bowl. Add the wine, onions, celery, and carrots, cover, and marinate in the refrigerator for about 24 hours.

Remove the meat from the marinade and pat dry with paper towels. Strain the vegetables and set the vegetables and wine aside separately.

In a large saucepan over medium heat, warm the oil and butter. Add the beef and cook, turning to brown on all sides, for about 10 minutes. Add the reserved vegetables, one-fourth of the reserved wine, and salt to taste. Cover and cook over low heat until very tender, about 4 hours. During this time turn the meat about 4 times and add the remaining wine, a little at a time, so that the pan is always moist.

When the meat is done, remove from the pan and keep warm.

Pour the contents of the pan into a food processor fitted with a metal blade and purée, or pass through a food mill. For a sauce with more texture, use the hand blender to whisk the cooking juices and vegetables together directly in the saucepan.

Reheat the puréed sauce and reduce over high heat if too thin. Slice the meat, arrange on a heated platter, pour on the sauce, and serve immediately.

Serves 6

Fricassea d'Agnello

Lamb Fricassée with Fresh Tarragon

¼ cup (2 oz/60 g) unsalted butter
3½ lb (1.8 kg) lamb, preferably from upper leg only, cut into bite-sized pieces
salt and freshly ground pepper
1 stalk celery, cut into pieces
1 carrot, cut into pieces
1 onion, cut into pieces
1 handful of fresh flat-leaf (Italian) parsley
1 fresh sprig rosemary
½ cup (4 fl oz/120 ml) dry white wine
⅓ cup (3 fl oz/90 ml) light meat stock
3 egg yolks
⅓ cup (3 fl oz/90 ml) milk
2 tablespoons fresh lemon juice
1 tablespoon minced fresh tarragon or flat-leaf (Italian) parsley

In a large saucepan over medium heat, melt the butter. Add the lamb and cook, stirring occasionally, until golden brown, about 10 minutes. Season to taste with salt and pepper and add the vegetables, parsley, rosemary, and wine. Lower the heat and cook uncovered, stirring occasionally, about 1½ hours.

▨ Remove the pan from the heat and discard the vegetables and herbs.

▨ To make the sauce, in a bowl whisk together the egg yolks, milk, stock, and lemon juice. Add to the lamb and stir well. Return the pan to low heat and cook, stirring, until slightly thickened. Remove from the heat and stir in the tarragon or parsley. Arrange on a heated platter and serve hot.

Serves 6

Costolette di Maiale alle Prugne

Pork Chops with Prunes

This recipe from the Friuli region has an Austrian influence. The chops take only a few minutes to prepare and should be cooked at the last minute. To serve a more elegant dish, top each chop with a thin, cooked apple ring with the prune set in the center.

2 prunes, pitted and softened if necessary
2 thin slices bacon, preferably Canadian bacon
1 tablespoon extra-virgin olive oil
½ tablespoon unsalted butter
2 pork chops, about 8 oz (240 g) each
¼ cup (2 fl oz/60 ml) dry white wine
1 teaspoon coarse-grain mustard
salt and freshly ground pepper

Preheat an oven to 350°F (180°C).
▣ Wrap each prune in a bacon slice and arrange on a sheet of aluminum foil. Place in the preheated oven until the bacon is crisp and golden, about 10 minutes.
▣ Meanwhile, in a frying pan over high heat, warm the oil and butter. Add the chops and cook for 3 minutes on each side. Add the wine, mustard, and salt and pepper to taste and stir into the pan juices.
▣ Arrange the chops on a heated platter, pour on the sauce, garnish with the prunes, and serve immediately.

Serves 2

I CONTORNI

Vegetables

In Italian, the word *contorni* means to surround. *Contorni* also means vegetable course because Italians always serve their vegetables surrounding the meat or fish of the *secondo piatto*. Italy's fertile soil and sunny, mild climate have assured Italians an abundance of high-quality vegetables from which to create their *contorni*. Indeed, the gardens of Italy are so prolific that the culinary possibilities are limited only by the cook's imagination.

Although many vegetables grace the Italian table, perhaps the most glorious of them all is the tomato. This versatile native of South America, which did not arrive in Italy until the sixteenth century, is often made into a sauce for a *contorno*, such as *peperoni alla marinara* in which it cloaks sweet peppers. When I was a child, the smell of simmering tomato sauce, fragrant with garlic, onion, and basil, would welcome me home from school and lift my spirits instantly. I was always ready to sneak a chunk of bread and dip it into the sauce.

Members of the Brassica family of vegetables, which include cauliflower, broccoli, cabbage, and a basketful of other greens, appear frequently in the role of *contorno*. Spinach and Swiss chard (silverbeet) often appear as well, sometimes lightly sautéed and crowned with simple toppings, such as *spinaci agli amaretti*, in which the greens are strewn with crushed almond cookies, or *bietole al pangrattato*, chard sprinkled with crisp, golden fried bread crumbs.

Artichokes are a particular favorite of Italians. In the countryside, their stark purplish green silhouettes, sometimes the only vegetable left in the winter garden, are a characteristic sight. Commonly harvested when very young, they are sometimes trimmed to bite-sized mouthfuls and eaten raw, dipped in extra-virgin olive oil and sprinkled with salt. More mature artichokes can be stuffed with a filling, such as the aromatic herb mixture in *carciofi ripieni di erbe*.

In Italy, blanching, the piling of earth around a vegetable as it grows to prevent light from turning it green, is customarily employed when cultivating celery, Belgian endive (chicory/witloof), and fennel. The practice produces vegetables with a more delicate taste and texture that marry especially well with other flavors, such as fennel cloaked in anchovy sauce or Belgian endive with walnuts.

Clearly, Italy has a venerable heritage of vegetable recipes. But it is the taste, texture, and freshness of the vegetables themselves that is the most important aspect of every dish. The best Italian cooks are careful never to disguise the exquisite natural qualities of their garden-fresh bounty.

Patate Arrosto

Roasted Potatoes

2½ lb (1.2 kg) boiling potatoes
1 cup (8 fl oz/240 ml) extra-virgin olive oil
1 sprig fresh rosemary
1 clove garlic
salt

Peel the potatoes and cut into 1-in (2.5-cm) cubes. Dry well with a cloth towel. Pour the oil into a cast-iron frying pan and heat to 340°F (170°C), or almost to the smoking point.

▨ Add the potatoes, rosemary, and garlic clove. Cook over medium heat, stirring occasionally, until the color of toasted nuts, about 20 minutes. Remove and discard the garlic and rosemary and drain the potatoes briefly on paper towels. Immediately arrange on a heated platter and serve.

Nastri di Carote e Zucchine

Carrot and Zucchini Ribbons

6 carrots
9 zucchini (courgettes)
3 tablespoons extra-virgin olive oil
salt and freshly ground pepper
1 tablespoon minced fresh flat-leaf (Italian) parsley

Using a food processor fitted with the slicing blade or a vegetable peeler, cut the carrots into thin lengthwise strips. Cut the green skin of the zucchini in the same way, reserving the flesh for another use. Put the vegetable ribbons in ice water to crisp.

▨ Drain the vegetables and pat dry. In a large frying pan over medium heat, warm the oil. Add the vegetables, season to taste with salt and pepper, and sauté until tender, about 3 minutes. Arrange the vegetables on a heated platter, sprinkle with the parsley, and serve immediately.

Each recipe serves 6

Clockwise from top left: Fennel in Anchovy Sauce, Roasted Potatoes, Carrot and Zucchini Ribbons, Artichokes with Fresh Herbs

Carciofi Ripieni di Erbe

Artichokes with Fresh Herbs

Artichokes grow well in temperate climates. They are lovely in gardens, where their purple flowers and magnificent foliage are always appreciated. This same recipe can be used for zucchini (courgettes), onions, or tomatoes.

2 slices coarse-textured bread, crusts removed
1 cup (8 fl oz/240 ml) milk
6 large globe artichokes
juice of 1 lemon
1 tablespoon minced fresh chives
1 tablespoon chopped fresh marjoram or basil
1 tablespoon chopped fresh flat-leaf (Italian) parsley
3 tablespoons freshly grated Parmesan cheese
1 anchovy fillet in oil, drained
1 egg
⅓ cup (3 fl oz/90 ml) extra-virgin olive oil
salt and freshly ground pepper
3 tablespoons water

In a bowl soak the bread in the milk for about 10 minutes.

▦ Meanwhile, fill a large bowl with cold water and add the lemon juice. Cut off the stems from the artichokes, pull off the tough outer leaves, cut off the tops, and remove the chokes. Pull the leaves apart slightly and then drop into the water, to prevent discoloring.

▦ Drain the bread, squeeze dry, and crumble into a mixing bowl. Add the herbs, Parmesan, anchovy, egg, and half of the oil and mix well. Season to taste with salt and pepper.

▦ Drain the artichokes and stuff them with the bread mixture, pushing it in between the layers of leaves. Pour the remaining oil and the water into a saucepan and arrange the artichokes upright in the pan. Cover and cook over low heat until tender, about 15 minutes.

▦ Arrange the artichokes on a platter and serve hot or at room temperature.

Serves 6

Finocchi all'Acciuga

Fennel in Anchovy Sauce

Fennel, originally from the south of Italy, is eaten raw as well as cooked, usually thinly sliced. Considered beneficial for digestion, it has a sweet and refreshing taste, especially when raw in salad. It grows above ground, but is always covered with mounds of earth to keep it white and tender. The veins should be hardly visible from the outside; if they are prominent, the bulb will be tough.

6 fennel bulbs
2 tablespoons extra-virgin olive oil
3 anchovy fillets in oil, drained
¾ cup (6 fl oz/180 ml) heavy (double) cream
salt and freshly ground pepper
½ cup (2 oz/60 g) freshly grated Parmesan cheese

Have a large bowl of ice water ready. Bring a large saucepan of salted water to a boil, add the fennel, and blanch for 5 minutes. Drain and place in the ice water, to prevent discoloring. Drain again and cut in quarters lengthwise. Cut off the root end and stems from the bulbs.

In a large pan over low heat, warm the oil. Add the anchovies and fry until they melt, a couple of minutes. Stir in the cream and add the fennel. Cover and cook over low heat until tender, about 10 minutes.

Arrange the fennel on a serving dish.

Reduce the sauce slightly over medium heat and season to taste with salt and pepper. Pour over the fennel, sprinkle with the Parmesan, and serve immediately.

Serves 6

Involtini di Lattuga

Lettuce Rolls

These rolls can be filled with different raw or cooked meats, sausage, *prosciutto* or *mortadella*, cooked vegetables, or fish. The covering can also be made with the blanched leaves of Swiss chard (silverbeet) or Savoy cabbage. You can prepare the rolls in advance and cook them for a few minutes just before serving.

1 slice coarse-textured bread, crust removed
½ cup (4 fl oz/120 ml) milk
6 large leaves Boston (butterhead) lettuce
2 oz (60 g) *mortadella*, finely chopped
1 egg yolk
2 ½ cups (5 oz/150 g) blanched broccoli florets
2 tablespoons freshly grated Parmesan cheese
salt and freshly ground pepper
2 tablespoons extra-virgin olive oil

In a bowl soak the bread in the milk for about 10 minutes. Drain, squeeze dry, and set aside.

▣ Have a large bowl of ice water ready. Bring a large saucepan of salted water to a boil and drop in the lettuce leaves. Using a slotted spoon, remove immediately to the ice water. Drain again and follow the step-by-step instructions for forming the rolls on the facing page.

▣ In a large, deep frying pan over low heat, warm the oil. Place the rolls, seam-side down, in the pan, cover, and cook for 5 minutes, turning once.

▣ Arrange the rolls on a heated platter and serve immediately.

Serves 6

1. On a flat work surface covered with a cloth, spread the blanched lettuce leaves so that the ribbed ends are closest to you. Press the ribs down with a knife blade to soften them. In a food processor fitted with the metal blade, combine the *mortadella*, egg yolk, bread, broccoli, and Parmesan. Process until well mixed, then season to taste with salt and pepper.

2. Spoon a line of filling across the middle of each leaf. Fold the sides of the leaf over the ends of the filling.

3. Starting from the stem end, roll up each lettuce leaf to enclose the filling completely.

Broccoli alla Salsiccia

Broccoli with Sausage

Broccoli is typically used in winter dishes. A southern vegetable, it is especially popular in Apulia, where great quantities are cultivated. Florets of green or white cauliflower can be substituted in this dish.

2 lb (900 g) broccoli
3 tablespoons extra-virgin olive oil
10 oz (300 g) sweet Italian sausage, casings removed and meat crumbled
½ cup (4 fl oz/120 ml) dry white wine
salt and freshly ground pepper

Cut off the florets from the broccoli and set aside. Discard the larger stems and cut the smaller stems into chunks. Have 2 bowls of ice water ready. Bring a saucepan of salted water to a boil. Add the stems and blanch for 1 minute. Lift out with a slotted spoon and transfer to a bowl of ice water, to halt the cooking. Repeat with the florets, putting them in the second bowl. Drain the stems and florets and set aside separately.

◼ In a large saucepan over medium heat, warm the oil. Add the sausage and cook, stirring constantly, for about 5 minutes. Add the broccoli stems and wine, cover, reduce the heat to low, and cook, stirring occasionally, for 10 minutes. Add the florets and cook for 2 more minutes. Season to taste with salt and pepper.

◼ Arrange the broccoli on a heated platter and serve immediately.

Serves 6

From top to bottom: Broccoli with Sausage, Leeks with Saffron, Green Beans with Toasted Hazelnuts, Bell Peppers with Tomato, Garlic and Basil Sauce

Fagiolini alle Nocciole

Green Beans with Toasted Hazelnuts

⅔ cup (3 oz/90 g) hazelnuts (filberts), roughly chopped
2 lb (900 g) green (string) beans
⅓ cup (3 fl oz/90 ml) extra-virgin olive oil

Preheat an oven to 350°F (180°C) and toast the hazelnuts until they begin to color, about 5 minutes. Set aside.

▦ Blanch the beans in boiling salted water for 1 minute. Drain, drop into a bowl of ice water, and drain again. In a large saucepan over low heat, cook them in the oil for about 10 minutes.

▦ Arrange the beans in a serving dish, sprinkle with the nuts, and serve immediately.

Peperoni alla Marinara

Bell Peppers with Tomato, Garlic, and Basil Sauce

⅓ cup (3 fl oz/90 ml) extra-virgin olive oil
6 yellow bell peppers (capsicums), cut in half lengthwise, seeded, and deribbed
3 cloves garlic, diced
1 lb (450 g) plum (egg) tomatoes, peeled and chopped, or canned with their liquid
salt and freshly ground pepper
1 handful of fresh basil leaves, shredded by hand

Preheat an oven to 350°F (180°C). Brush a baking dish with half of the oil and place the peppers in it, cut-side up. Cook in the preheated oven for 20 minutes. Meanwhile, in a saucepan, sauté the garlic in the remaining oil until translucent, about 3 minutes. Add the tomatoes and cook over medium heat, stirring occasionally, until liquid evaporates, about 15 minutes. Season with salt and pepper.

▦ Arrange the peppers, cut-side up, on a platter; sprinkle with salt, and fill with the sauce. Sprinkle with the basil and serve hot.

Each recipe serves 6

Porri allo Zafferano

Leeks with Saffron

To be certain one is getting true saffron, buy it in thread form rather than powder, which may be adulterated. Saffron is used in many dishes, among them the famed fragrant, yellow *risotto alla milanese*. Before using, saffron needs to be soaked in a little hot stock or water for about five minutes. This recipe can also be used for fennel, onions, green (spring) onions, or asparagus in place of the leeks, and minced parsley may replace the saffron.

4 lb (1.8 kg) leeks
1 cup (8 fl oz/240 ml) heavy (double) cream
1 large pinch of saffron threads or 2 tablespoons minced fresh flat-leaf (Italian) parsley
½ cup (2 oz/60 g) freshly grated Parmesan cheese
salt

Cut off and discard the green parts of the leeks. Cut in half lengthwise, gently open the leaves, and rinse under cold water.

◻ Bring a saucepan of salted water to a gentle boil. Add the leeks, and blanch for 2 minutes. Drain and place in a large frying pan.

◻ Heat ¼ cup (2 fl oz/60 ml) of the cream in a small saucepan, remove from the heat, and add the saffron; steep for 5 minutes. Add the remaining cream and the Parmesan cheese to the saffron mixture and pour over the leeks. Cook, uncovered, over low heat until tender, about 5 minutes. (If you are omitting the saffron, simply combine the cream, Parmesan cheese, and parsley and pour over the leeks.)

◻ Season to taste with salt, arrange the leeks on a heated platter, and serve.

Serves 6

Melanzane all'Agro

Sweet-and-Sour Eggplant

In the past eggplants (aubergines) had a very strong taste, so they had to be salted and weighted to extract the bitterness. Modern cultivating methods make this step no longer necessary. This recipe can be prepared up to the point where the tomato is added, then covered and refrigerated for up to three hours. Reheat and add the tomato just before serving.

3 tablespoons extra-virgin olive oil
½ onion, sliced
2 eggplants (aubergines), about 10 oz (300 g) total weight, unpeeled and diced
2 bay leaves
¼ cup (1 oz/30 g) raisins, softened in water to cover for about 30 minutes and drained
¼ cup (2 fl oz/60 ml) red wine vinegar
½ cup (4 fl oz/120 ml) water
1 tomato, peeled, and diced
salt and freshly ground pepper

In a large frying pan over medium heat, warm the oil. Add the onion and eggplants and sauté, stirring occasionally, for about 10 minutes. Add the bay leaves, raisins, and vinegar. Cover, reduce the heat, and cook until the vinegar evaporates, about 10 minutes. Add the water, a little at a time, and continue cooking for 30 minutes.
Remove and discard the bay leaves, add the tomato, and season to taste with salt and pepper. Stir briefly to mix well and serve immediately.

Serves 6

From the top: Swiss Chard with Fried Bread Crumbs, Sweet-and-Sour Eggplant, Caramelized Carrots

Carote Caramellate

Caramelized Carrots

This is a recipe from the Renaissance, when vegetables were often served in sweet-and-sour sauces. Pearl onions, celeriac (celery root), or zucchini (courgettes) can be prepared in the same way.

2½ lb (1.2 kg) carrots, trimmed
3 tablespoons extra-virgin olive oil
salt and freshly ground pepper
⅓ cup (3 oz/90 g) sugar
⅓ cup (3 fl oz/90 ml) red wine vinegar
3 tablespoons raisins, softened in water to cover for about 30 minutes and drained

Using a food processor fitted with the slicing blade, cut the carrots into slices about ⅛ in (3 mm) thick.

▣ In a frying pan over low heat, warm the oil. Add the carrots and cook, stirring occasionally, about 10 minutes. Season to taste with salt and pepper, add the sugar, and continue to cook for another 5 minutes. Add the vinegar and raisins, stir well, and cook for 2 more minutes.

▣ Arrange the carrots on a platter and serve immediately.

Serves 6

Bietole al Pangrattato
Swiss Chard with Fried Bread Crumbs

Swiss chard (silverbeet) makes both an excellent vegetable dish and pasta sauce. Cauliflower, both green and white, can be cooked in the same way.

2½ lb (1.2 kg) Swiss chard (silverbeet)
⅓ cup (3 fl oz/90 ml) extra-virgin olive oil
3 cloves garlic, minced
1 anchovy fillet in oil, drained (optional)
½ cup (2 oz/60 g) fine dry bread crumbs
3 tablespoons raisins, softened in water to cover for about 30 minutes and drained
3 tablespoons pine nuts

Remove the ribs from the Swiss chard and peel them. Have a large bowl of ice water ready. Bring a large saucepan of salted water to a boil, add the ribs and cook for 3 minutes. Add the leaves and cook for 1 minute. Drain and place in the ice water to halt the cooking. Drain again, squeeze dry and chop roughly.

In a saucepan over low heat, warm half of the oil. Add the garlic and anchovy, if using, and cook until the garlic is translucent, about 3 minutes. Add the chard, cover and cook, stirring occasionally, for 5 minutes.

Meanwhile, pour the remaining oil into a frying pan over medium heat. Add the bread crumbs and sauté, stirring continuously, until golden or about 3 minutes. Add the raisins and stir well.

Arrange the chard on a platter and sprinkle with the pine nuts. To serve, spoon onto individual plates and, at the last minute, sprinkle with the bread crumbs.

Serves 6

From the top: Spinach with Macaroons, Belgian Endive with Walnuts

Indivia del Belgio alle Noci

Belgian Endive with Walnuts

2 tablespoons extra-virgin olive oil
6 Belgian endives (witloof/chicory), trimmed and halved lengthwise
¼ cup (2 fl oz/60 ml) dry white wine
½ cup (2 oz/60 g) freshly grated Parmesan cheese
⅔ cup (2 oz/60 g) walnuts, chopped
salt

Pour the oil into a large frying pan and add the endives, cut-side down. Pour the wine over and sprinkle with salt. Cover, and cook over low heat until tender, about 5 minutes.

▦ Arrange the endives, cut-side up, on a heated platter. Sprinkle with the Parmesan and walnuts and serve immediately.

Spinaci agli Amaretti

Spinach with Macaroons

The spinach in Italy has large, curly leaves. It is not necessary to remove the stalks, which, like the leaves, cook quickly. When fresh, spinach leaves should be shiny and crisp. You can also make croquettes, hash, or puddings with this mixture, or you can substitute Swiss chard, onions, broccoli, or cauliflower for the spinach.

2½ lbs (1.2 kg) fresh spinach
3 tablespoons extra-virgin olive oil
salt
12 *amaretti* (imported Italian macaroons), crumbled

Have a large bowl of ice water ready. Bring a saucepan of salted water to a boil, add the spinach, and blanch for 2 minutes. Drain and put into the ice water. Drain again and squeeze.

▦ In a heavy pan over medium heat, warm the oil. Add the spinach, cover, and cook, stirring occasionally, for 3 minutes. Season to taste with salt.

▦ Arrange the spinach on a heated platter. Sprinkle with the *amaretti* and serve immediately.

Each recipe serves 6

Tortini di Patate

Potato Cakes

This is an elegant way to serve vegetables. The circles look like flowers and are attractive placed around meat or fish. Use your imagination with the *tortini*—contrast colors and make different designs; alternate potato and tomato or tomato and zucchini (courgette) slices. Onion slices will add even more flavor, and the vegetables can be dressed with such herbs as sage, thyme, tarragon, mint, and oregano.

6 large baking potatoes, peeled
3 tablespoons extra-virgin olive oil
salt and freshly ground pepper
1 tablespoon finely chopped fresh rosemary

Preheat an oven to 350°F (180°C). Using a food processor fitted with the slicing blade, slice the potatoes thinly. Brush the slices with half of the oil and sprinkle to taste with salt and pepper.

▣ Brush a baking sheet with the remaining oil. Arrange the potato slices in 6 rounds, overlapping the slices and making each cake about 5 in (12 cm) in diameter. Sprinkle with rosemary and bake in the preheated oven until golden but not too dark, about 10 minutes. Remove with a spatula to a heated platter and serve hot.

▣ These potato cakes can be cooked up to 6 hours in advance and kept at room temperature. Five minutes before serving, reheat them.

Serves 6

I DOLCI

Desserts

Italians have a long tradition of fine confectionary. Pastries and cakes are always served for special occasions, such as weddings and religious holidays, and are sometimes enjoyed for a mid-morning or mid-afternoon snack at a bar or a *pasticceria*, a bakery that specializes in the making of sweets.

Among the many delicious *dolci* for which the Italians are renowned are *montebianco*, fluffy chestnut purée beneath a cap of whipped cream; *buccellato*, an anise-flavored ring cake popularly baked in winter; *frittelle*, crisp, light rice fritters traditionally served on Saint Joseph's Day; and *panforte*, or "strong bread," the dense, spiced cake of Siena. But these sweets are seldom eaten at the end of an everyday meal; a piece of fruit is by far the most popular final course.

Many of the desserts in the following pages are very light and will complement most meals, however. Fruits are the bases for a number of them. Fresh grapes rest on a custard-lined tart shell in *crostata di uva*, and poached peaches are infused with the flavor of almonds in *pesche agli amaretti*. *Macedonia di arance*, named for a region in southern Europe, is a classic recipe for lightly caramelizing fruits, while *albicocche alla grappa* pairs dried apricots with Italy's famed smooth yet fiery brandy.

Creamy ricotta is lightly whipped and topped with streams of fragrant honey, or laced with coffee and used to fill thin, crisp pastry shells for *cannoli*. Freshly brewed *espresso* also flavors *panna cotta al caffè*, small molds of gently cooked cream.

For a truly simple finish to a meal, plain *espresso* can be served, with or without a topping of hot and frothy steamed milk. Or the *espresso* can be blended with chocolate in *caffè alla cioccolata* or mixed with a splash of *grappa*.

From the top: Mocha Coffee, Apricots Soaked in Grappa

Albicocche alla Grappa

Apricots Soaked in Grappa

This is always a winter dish, and is also delicious when made with dried figs.

6 pitted, dried apricots
½ cup (4 fl oz/120 ml) good-quality *grappa* or brandy
1 handful of fresh mint leaves, optional

Put the apricots in a bowl, pour in the *grappa* to cover completely, and set aside at room temperature for at least 15 days, stirring occasionally. During that time the strong flavor of the *grappa* will mellow, sweetened by the natural sugars in the fruit.

To serve, divide the apricots and their marinade between 2 individual dessert bowls. Decorate with the mint.

Serves 2

Caffè alla Cioccolata

Mocha Coffee

½ cup (4 fl oz/120 ml) heavy (double) cream
6 tablespoons (1½ oz/45 g) cocoa powder
6 servings *espresso* coffee, brewed according to manufacturer's directions
4 cups (32 fl oz/1 l) milk

Using a hand blender, whip the cream until stiff peaks form; set aside.

Put the cocoa in a small saucepan. Over low heat gradually stir in the coffee, mixing until creamy. Add the milk and heat, stirring, until almost at a boil.

Divide the coffee mixture among 6 cups, top each cup with a spoonful of whipped cream, and serve immediately.

Serves 6

Grappa is a distilled spirit made from *vinaccia* or pomace— the skins, seeds, and stems that remain at the end of a wine crush. The pomace is boiled in copper stills, producing a clear liquor that has a pleasant barklike flavor and packs a bracing 90-proof punch. *Grappa* is considered a *digestivo,* consumed at the end of a large meal to stimulate digestion. It may stimulate lively conversation as well; taken in small amounts, *grappa* has a decided tonic effect. *Grappa* may also appear at any time of the day in what Italians politely call *caffè corretto—espresso* corrected (spiked) with a shot of *grappa,* making it a potent pick-me-up.

Crostata di Uva

Grape Tart

⅔ cup (5 oz/150 g) unsalted butter, plus 1 tablespoon for pan
⅔ cup (5 oz/150 g) sugar
2 cups (8 oz/240 g) plus 1 tablespoon all-purpose (plain) flour
3 egg yolks
2 tablespoons plus ¾ cup (7 fl oz/210 ml) milk
1 teaspoon grated lemon zest
10 oz (300 g) seedless white or red grapes

To make the tart shell, combine the butter, half the sugar, 2 cups flour, 1 egg yolk, the 2 tablespoons milk, and lemon zest in a food processor fitted with the metal blade. Process until all of the ingredients are incorporated and a rough dough forms. Form the dough into a ball, wrap in plastic wrap, and refrigerate for 2 hours.

▣ Preheat an oven to 350°F (180°C). Let the dough come to room temperature and roll it out on a lightly floured board into a 10-in (25-cm) round. Coat a 9-in (23-cm) tart pan with removable bottom with 1 tablespoon butter and then dust with flour. Line with the dough, cutting the top off even with the pan rim. Using a fork poke holes in the bottom of the shell and place in the preheated oven. After about 10 minutes the dough will rise slightly. Remove from the oven and, with the palm of your hand, press the dough down. Return the pan to the oven and bake until golden brown, about 20 minutes. Allow to cool completely before filling.

▣ To make the filling, combine the remaining 2 egg yolks and the remaining sugar in the top pan of a double boiler over simmering water and whip until light with a hand blender. Add the 1 tablespoon flour and the remaining milk, a little at a time, and cook, whisking continuously, until thick enough to coat the back of a spoon. Do not boil. Set aside to cool.

▣ To assemble the tart, place the cooled crust on a serving platter and pour the custard into it. Cover the top with the grapes and serve immediately.

Serves 6

Clockwise from top left: Grape Tart, Cappuccino, Chocolate Cake with Coffee Zabaglione, Coffee Laced with Grappa

Caffè con Grappa
Coffee Laced with Grappa

This is a coffee for serving after lunch or dinner, for a particularly merry occasion. *Grappa* is usually drunk with *espresso*, but it can be added to regular brewed coffee as long as the coffee is served black.

1 serving *espresso* coffee brewed according to manufacturer's directions
1 tablespoon *grappa* or brandy, or to taste

Immediately pour the *grappa* in the *espresso* and serve.

Serves 1

Cappuccino
Coffee with Steamed Milk

6 servings *espresso* coffee brewed according to manufacturer's directions
2 cups (16 fl oz/480 ml) milk
1 tablespoon cocoa powder, optional

Pour each *espresso* serving in a regular-sized coffee cup.
▨ Pour the milk into a metal pitcher. Place the vapor tube of the coffee machine into the milk and inject the milk with a stream of very hot, highly compressed air. Immediately divide the hot, foamy milk among six coffee cups. Sprinkle each serving with cocoa powder, if using, by passing it through a fine sieve.

Serves 6

The mighty Venetian republic was born of commerce. Its earliest mercantile power came from salt extracted from the surrounding lagoon, and by the ninth century the Venetians had monopolized the salt trade in the northeastern Mediterranean. As their wealth grew, they entered into the nascent spice trade – first with pepper and then with a long list of spices. They established a far-flung empire and basked in its wealth. When their spice trade monopoly was challenged by Portugal, the Venetians shifted to the import of coffee and established the earliest coffee houses. Today, this legacy continues in the rococo splendor of Venice's Caffè Florian.

Moro in Camicia

Chocolate Cake with Coffee Zabaglione

½ cup (4 oz/120 g) unsalted butter, plus 1 tablespoon for mold
½ cup (3 oz/90 g) almonds, toasted and finely chopped
6 squares (6 oz/180 g) semisweet (plain) chocolate
6 large eggs separated, plus 3 egg yolks and 1 egg white if serving cold
1¼ cups (10 oz/300 g) sugar
⅓ cup (3 fl oz/90 ml) *espresso* coffee brewed according to manufacturer's directions

Preheat an oven to 350°F (180°C). To make the cake, coat a deep mold about 6 in (15 cm) in diameter with 1 tablespoon butter. Carefully coat it with some of the almonds and then refrigerate.

▣ In the top pan of a double boiler over simmering water, melt the chocolate with the remaining butter, stirring frequently. Let the mixture cool completely.

▣ Using a hand blender, beat the 6 egg whites in a bowl until stiff peaks form.

▣ In another bowl, beat together ¾ cup plus 2 tablespoons (7 oz/210 g) sugar and 6 of the egg yolks until light and fluffy. Mix in the melted chocolate and beat until creamy. Using a spatula gently fold in the beaten egg whites and the remaining almonds. Pour the batter into the prepared mold and bake in the preheated oven until a toothpick inserted in the center comes out dry, about 40 minutes. Let cool in the pan.

▣ To make the *zabaglione*, combine the remaining 3 egg yolks and the remaining sugar in the top pan of a double boiler over simmering water. Using a hand blender, beat until fluffy. Add the coffee and, whisking constantly, cook gently until thick and foamy. Do not boil.

▣ To assemble the dessert, run a knife blade around the edge of the mold and invert the cake onto a serving dish. Pour the hot sauce over and serve immediately.

▣ This dessert can also be served cold. Unmold the cake and allow to cool. Set the cooked sauce aside and, when it is cold, fold in a stiffly beaten egg white. Just before serving, pour the sauce over the cake.

Serves 6

Tiramisù

Tuscan Trifle

Tiramisù is now known all over the world. Originally it was called *zuppa del duca* (the duke's soup) and was created in honor of a visit by Grand Duke Cosimo de' Medici III to Siena. The Grand Duke took the recipe home to Florence, where it became popular in the English intellectual and artistic colony by the end of the nineteenth century. They, in turn, took it to England and the dish is now also known in Italy as *zuppa Inglese*. My version is quite light.

4 squares (4 oz/120 g) semisweet (plain) chocolate
3 egg yolks
3 tablespoons sugar
1¼ cups (10 fl oz/300 ml) Vin Santo or other dessert wine
1 egg white
¼ cup (2 fl oz/60 ml) very strong *espresso* coffee brewed according to
    manufacturer's directions
1 cup (8 oz/240 g) ricotta, at room temperature
1 cup (8 fl oz/240 ml) heavy (double) cream
4 oz (120 g) ladyfingers (sponge fingers)
1 tablespoon instant-coffee powder

In the top pan of a double boiler over simmering water, melt the chocolate. Let cool completely.

▣ To make the *zabaglione* and assemble the *tiramisù*, follow the step-by-step directions on the facing page.

▣ To decorate, place the reserved whipped cream in a pastry (forcing) bag fitted with a fluted tip and pipe it on top. At this point the *tiramisù* may be refrigerated for up to 12 hours. Sprinkle the coffee powder on top just before serving.

Serves 6

1. To make the *zabaglione*, using a hand blender, beat the egg yolks with the sugar in the top pan of a double boiler until frothy and light. Add ½ cup (4 fl oz/120 ml) of the wine, place over gently simmering water, and whip until the mixture begins to thicken. Do not let it boil. Remove from the heat, fold in the cooled chocolate, and let cool completely.

2. Beat the egg white until stiff peaks form and, using a spatula, fold it into the cooled *zabaglione*. Stir together the *espresso* and ricotta and set the mixture aside. Whip the cream until stiff peaks form.

3. Dip the ladyfingers into the remaining wine and arrange them on the bottom of a 9-in (23-cm) bowl. Cover with half of the ricotta mixture, then half of the *zabaglione,* and finally half of the whipped cream. Repeat the layers of ricotta mixture and *zabaglione* but reserve the remaining whipped cream.

Pesche agli Amaretti

Peaches with Almond Macaroons

The most delicious peaches are those with white flesh, but they are sometimes difficult to find. One can also make this dessert with apricots or, in winter, with pears.

18 *amaretti* (imported Italian macaroons)
½ cup (4 fl oz/120 ml) Frangelico (hazelnut) liqueur
6 peaches
1 cup (8 fl oz/240 ml) semisweet white wine
⅔ cup (5 oz/150 g) sugar
1 cup (8 fl oz/240 ml) heavy (double) cream, for decoration

In a bowl soften the *amaretti* in the liqueur and mix until creamy.
▣ Bring a saucepan of water to a boil. Add the peaches, blanch for 1 minute, and drain. Peel, halve, and remove and discard the pits. Arrange cut-side down in a large saucepan, and pour in the wine. Stir in the sugar, cover, and cook over low heat until just tender, about 10 minutes. Remove with a slotted spoon and set aside. Continue to simmer the liquid until reduced to ½ cup (4 fl oz/120 ml), then let cool completely.
▣ Using a hand blender, whip the cream until stiff peaks form.
▣ To assemble the dessert, arrange the peaches on a serving platter and top with the *amaretti* mixture. Pour the wine syrup around the peaches and decorate with the cream.

Serves 6

From the top: Hazelnut Cake, Peaches with Almond Macaroons, Cold Strawberry Mousse with Nougat

Torta di Nocciole

Hazelnut Cake

¾ cup (4 oz/120 g) almonds, blanched and toasted
½ cup (4 oz/120 g) unsalted butter, melted, plus 1 tablespoon for the pan
1 cup (8 oz/240 g) sugar
2 whole eggs plus 3 egg yolks
½ cup (2 oz/60 g) all-purpose (plain) flour, plus 2 tablespoons for the pan
1¼ cups (6 oz/180 g) hazelnuts (filberts), peeled
2 tablespoons water
¾ cup (6 fl oz/180 ml) heavy (double) cream

Preheat an oven to 340°F (170°C). Pulverize half of the almonds in a food processor fitted with the metal blade, using brief pulses. Remove and set aside.

▨ Combine the butter and ⅔ cup (5 oz/150 g) of the sugar in the food processor and process until soft and fluffy. With the machine running, add the eggs and egg yolks, one at a time, mixing well after each addition.

▨ Pour the egg mixture into a bowl and fold in the flour and ground almonds.

▨ Coat a 9-in (23-cm) springform pan with 1 tablespoon butter and dust with 2 tablespoons flour. Pour in the batter and smooth the surface with a spatula.

▨ Bake the cake in the preheated oven until a toothpick inserted in the center comes out dry, about 40 minutes. Let cool for a few minutes, then remove the pan sides, slide onto a platter, and let cool completely.

▨ Meanwhile, caramelize the hazelnuts. Pour the remaining ⅓ cup (3 oz/90 g) sugar into a small, heavy saucepan with the water and cook over medium heat, stirring constantly, for 3 minutes. Remove from the heat and add the hazelnuts, stirring constantly until completely coated. Return the pan to medium heat and stir until the hazelnuts caramelize. Pour out onto waxed paper and, using tongs or tweezers, separate them and let cool completely.

▨ To assemble, place the cake right-side up on a serving dish. Using a hand blender or a whisk, beat the cream until stiff peaks form. Spread a layer of cream over the top of the cake. Put the remaining cream in a pastry (forcing) bag fitted with a fluted tip and pipe rosettes onto the sides. Arrange the hazelnuts on the top in concentric circles, working from the center outward. Serve immediately.

Serves 6

Semifreddo di Fragole al Torrone

Cold Strawberry Mousse with Nougat

Since a *semifreddo*, or mousse, is usually made with whipped cream and straw-berries, chocolate, or other ingredients, it is usually quite rich. Ricotta substi-tuted for the cream makes it lighter. *Torrone* (nougat) is a specialty of Cremona that has spread throughout the country and is especially popular in Abruzzi and Sicily. Classic *torrone* is made with honey, almonds, and egg whites, to which hazelnuts, pistachios or candied fruit are added. The confection, which may be soft or hard, is generally sandwiched between wafers.

⅓ cup (3 oz/90 g) sugar
¼ cup (2 fl oz/60 ml) water
2 envelopes (2 teaspoons/½ oz/15 g) gelatin
1 tablespoon almond oil
1¼ lb (600 g) strawberries, hulled
1½ cups (12 oz/360 g) ricotta
6 oz (180 g) *torrone* (nougat)

In a small saucepan combine the sugar and the water and place over low heat, stirring until dissolved. Remove from the heat and sprinkle the gelatin over the top. Set aside to cool.

▨ Brush a 7-in (18-cm) mold with the almond oil. In a food processor fitted with the metal blade, purée the strawberries, or pass them through a food mill into a bowl. Add the gelatin mixture and the ricotta and process briefly or stir to blend. Pour the mixture into the prepared mold and refrigerate for 6 hours.

▨ To serve, dip the base of the mold into boiling water for about 5 seconds and invert onto a platter. In a food processor fitted with the metal blade, crumble the *torrone* with a few pulses. Sprinkle the candy over the mousse and serve.

Serves 6

Created in Cremona for the marriage of Bianca Maria Visconti and Francesco Sforza in 1471, *torrone* marks the joining of two of the most powerful noble houses in Italy. This nut-laden nougat was made to resemble the impressive Torrazzo in the center of the city, the tallest bell tower in all of Italy. It is a dense, rich mix of egg whites, honey, almonds, and often candied fruit, which cools to a tooth-cracking hardness. Modern versions often come gilded with a delicious and totally superfluous coating of bitter chocolate.

Torta della Nonna

Fruit Crumble Tart

This cake, made with a lot of fruit and little dough, is a wonderful dessert to accompany lunch. The crumble can be quickly made in a food processor, and you can use any fruit you like, although apple is common because it has little juice. This is an old recipe, having belonged to the grandmother of a dear friend of mine who made it for me often. For a richer presentation, serve with heavy (double) cream flavored with raspberry syrup.

⅓ cup (3 oz/90 g) sugar
6 tablespoons (3 oz/90 g) unsalted butter, at room temperature, plus 1 tablespoon for pan
1 extra-large egg
1 teaspoon baking powder
¾ cup (3 oz/90 g) ground almonds
2 cups (8 oz/240 g) all-purpose (plain) flour
4 Golden Delicious apples, peeled, cored, and grated
⅓ cup (2 oz/60 g) raisins, soaked in dry white wine to cover for about 30 minutes
    and drained
⅓ cup (2 oz/60 g) pine nuts
⅓ cup (4 oz/125 g) blackberry or blueberry jam
18 *amaretti* (imported Italian macaroons)

Preheat an oven to 350°F (180°C). Using a food processor fitted with the metal blade, cream together the sugar and butter until soft and fluffy. Add the egg, baking powder, ground almonds, and flour. Process with brief pulses until crumbly.

▣ In a bowl mix together the apples, raisins, pine nuts, jam, and *amaretti*.

▣ Coat an 8-in (20-cm) springform pan with the 1 tablespoon butter. Cover the bottom and sides with two-thirds of the crumbled dough, patting it firmly and evenly. Fill the shell with the apple mixture and sprinkle the top with the remaining crumbly dough.

▣ Bake in the preheated oven until set and crust is golden, about 1 hour. If the crumble starts to brown too much, cover the pan loosely with aluminum foil.

▣ To serve, remove the pan sides and slide onto a platter. Serve warm or at room temperature.

Serves 6

Pinolata

Pine Nut Cake

This cake is often encountered in Tuscany, where pine nuts are plentiful and not very costly. It is not a dish to end a meal, but rather one that is served for breakfast or brunch, or for *merenda,* a mid-morning or mid-afternoon snack.

1½ cups (6 oz/180 g) all-purpose (plain) flour, plus 3 tablespoons for the pan
1 teaspoon baking powder
pinch of salt
½ cup (4 oz/120 g) unsalted butter, at room temperature, plus 1 tablespoon
   for the pan
½ cup (4 oz/120 g) sugar
3 eggs
½ cup (3 oz/90 g) pine nuts

Preheat an oven to 350°F (180°C). Sift together the flour, baking powder, and salt into a bowl.

▣ Using a food processor fitted with the metal blade, or a hand blender, cream together the butter and sugar until soft and fluffy. Add the eggs, 1 at a time, and then mix in the flour mixture. The dough will be quite soft.

▣ Butter a loaf pan measuring about 12 by 6 in (30 by 15 cm) and dust with flour. Pour the dough into the pan and sprinkle with the pine nuts. Bake in the preheated oven until a toothpick inserted into the center comes out dry, about 40 minutes.

▣ Cool completely on a rack before serving, with or without a pitcher of cream on the side.

Serves 6–8

Clockwise from the top left: Coffee-Flavored Cooked Cream, Caramelized Orange Salad, Ricotta Topped with Honey, Pine Nut Cake

Panforte, another Tuscan confection, dates from medieval Siena, a city once known for its lucrative spice trade. In its earliest form, this sweet mix of honey, almonds, figs, and flour was known as *panis acidis—acidis* because it fermented quickly. Some enterprising baker added spices, including copious quantities of black pepper. These precious additions both stopped the fermenting and drove the price sky-high. Rechristened *panforte,* it kept for months, making it the perfect food for well-heeled crusaders. It may, however, have caused a dilemma for the most religious; spices were said to arouse earthly desires.

Panna Cotta al Caffè

Coffee-Flavored Cooked Cream

This simple dessert from Piedmont has recently become popular abroad. It can be flavored in different ways, with chocolate, cinnamon, lemon or orange zest, or strained fruits such as strawberries, raspberries, or blackberries. Once unmolded, it can be kept in the refrigerator for up to 12 hours undecorated or for up to 6 hours decorated. You can even make a large quantity, pour it into molds, and freeze them for up to three months. Let the cream come to room temperature before unmolding and serving.

1 small cup (about 4 fl oz/120 ml) very strong *espresso* coffee brewed according to
    manufacturer's directions
1 cup (8 fl oz/240 ml) heavy (double) cream
¼ cup (2 oz/60 g) sugar
1 envelope (1 teaspoon/¼ oz/7 g) unflavored powdered gelatin
coffee beans for decoration

Pour half of the cream into a saucepan, add the sugar and *espresso,* and heat almost to a boil. Remove from the heat and sprinkle the gelatin on top. Stir until the gelatin dissolves and let cool to room temperature, stirring occasionally.

▨ Using a hand blender, whip the remaining cream into soft peaks. Remove 6 tablespoons of the cream and whip them into stiff peaks. Place in a pastry (forcing) bag fitted with a fluted tip and put in the refrigerator. Using a spatula, gently fold the soft whipped cream into the gelatin mixture.

▨ Pour the cream mixture into 2 individual ring or round molds and refrigerate for about 3 hours.

▨ To serve, immerse the base of each mold in boiling water for about 5 seconds and invert onto individual serving plates. Using the pastry bag, pipe cream rosettes onto the molds, then decorate with the coffee beans.

Serves 2

Macedonia di Arance

Caramelized Orange Salad

7 oranges, preferably blood oranges
⅔ cup (5 oz/150 g) sugar
¼ cup (2 fl oz/60 ml) Grand Marnier liqueur

Peel 6 of the oranges. Cut the zest of 3 oranges into thin strips. Juice the remaining orange.
▦ Slice the peeled oranges crosswise and overlap the slices on an oval serving dish.
▦ Pour the sugar into a heavy-bottomed saucepan and cook over low heat, without stirring, until it begins to turn dark around the edges. Then stir it with a wooden spoon until the whole surface becomes foamy and turns a golden brown. Add the orange juice, orange zest, and liqueur. Remove from the heat and set aside to cool.
▦ Pour the cooled sauce over the orange slices.
▦ This dish can be prepared ahead and refrigerated for up to 6 hours before serving.

Serves 6

Ricotta al Miele

Ricotta Topped with Honey

Ricotta, which means "recooked," is the whey from cow's or sheep's milk cheese. Low in fat, especially when made with sheep's milk, ricotta should be kept refrigerated and eaten within two days of purchase.

1¼ cup (10 fl oz/300 ml) honey, preferably chestnut-flower honey
2½ cups (1¼ lb/600 g) ricotta
1 tablespoon fresh thyme flowers or thyme leaves

Heat the honey in a saucepan until it liquefies; keep warm. Divide the ricotta evenly among 6 individual dessert dishes or goblets. Pour some of the warmed honey over each serving, sprinkle decoratively with the thyme, and serve immediately.

Serves 6

Cannoli alla Ricotta

Cannoli with Ricotta and Coffee

One of the most traditional of all Sicilian desserts, *cannoli* are now popular throughout Italy, but especially in the southern regions. *Cannoli* can also be filled with coffee- or chocolate-flavored cream or a simple custard of egg yolk, a little flour, and milk. This recipe is adapted from a book by Sicilian food authority Pino Correnti. *Cannoli* must be filled at the last minute or the shells will become soggy.

1¼ cups (5 oz/150 g) all-purpose (plain) flour, plus flour for working
2 teaspoons sugar
1 tablespoon cocoa powder
2 tablespoons *espresso* coffee brewed according to manufacturer's directions
1 egg white
1 tablespoon lard (pork fat), melted, or 1 tablespoon oil, warmed slightly
5 cups (40 fl oz/1.2 l) oil for deep-frying
1 cup (8 oz/240 g) ricotta
½ cup (3 oz/90 g) confectioners (icing) sugar
½ teaspoon instant-coffee powder
2 squares (2 oz/60 g) semisweet (plain) chocolate, cut into small pieces

To make the *cannoli*, put the flour into a bowl. Make a well in the center, and pour in the sugar, cocoa powder, *espresso*, egg white, and the slightly warm lard or oil. Using a fork, gradually pull in the walls of the well and stir until all the ingredients come together in a rough dough. Alternatively, combine the ingredients in a food processor fitted with the plastic blade and process with light pulses until a rough dough forms.

▨ Knead the dough on a lightly floured board until firm and smooth but not too dry. Shape into a ball, wrap in plastic wrap, and refrigerate for about 2 hours.

▨ To shape and cook the *cannoli*, follow the step-by-step instructions on the facing page, using the oil for frying.

▨ To make the filling, in a bowl mix together the ricotta, confectioners sugar, and coffee powder and stir in the chocolate pieces. Using a pastry (forcing) bag fitted with a plain tip ¾ in (2 cm) in diameter, pipe the filling into the *cannoli* shells. Serve immediately.

Serves 6

1. On a lightly floured work surface, roll out the dough into a sheet about ⅛ in (2 mm) thick. Cut into 4-in (9-cm) squares.

2. Wrap each square around a metal *cannoli* tube, wetting the edges lightly so that they form a secure seam.

3. In a deep frying pan, heat the oil to 340°F (170°C). Drop in the *cannoli*, a few at a time; do not crowd the pan. Cook until golden, about 5 minutes. Remove with a slotted utensil or tongs and drain on paper towels. Let cool, then slip the shells off of the tubes.

Acknowledgments

The de' Medici Kitchen television series would not have been possible without the participation of numerous companies and individuals in Italy and the U.S. to whom we are extremely grateful. I would especially like to thank the funder of the series, Braun, Inc., for their support of the project from its inception; as well as British Airways, The Parc 55 Hotel of San Francisco, Giorgio Armani, The Banfi Vintners Foundation, George V Imports, Greenleaf Produce, ITAL Foods, Crate&Barrel, Biordi Art Imports, Williams-Sonoma, and Sue Fisher King for production assistance.

The craftsmanship and artistry of the television staff are acknowledged on the screen, and I thank them all for their skill and vision. In addition, and in no particular order (since their contributions were equally valuable) thanks goes to the back kitchen: Bridget Charters, Carl Abbott, and Cathy Conner; to my staff Linda Brandt, Lisa Chaney, and Robert Steinberg; to director Bruce Franchini; to our set designer and stylists Craig Edelblut, Sandra Griswold, and Bernie Schimbke; to our coproducers on the Italy shoots, Michael Lerner and Shelley Handler, whose footage added immeasurably to the series; to our studio guests Carol Field, Carlo Middione and Guido Stucchi; and to all of Lorenza de' Medici's family and staff at Badia a Coltibuono for their patience and enthusiasm during the process of making television—which sometimes seems more medieval than the venerable abbey itself.

Peter L. Stein
Executive Producer, KQED

The Publishers would like to thank the following people and organizations for their assistance in making this book possible:

Norman Kolpas, Richard VanOosterhout, Sigrid Chase, Fee-ling Tan, Ruth Jacobson, Karen Richardson, Patty Hill, Laurie Wertz, Winnie Lum, Beverley Sharpe, Rapid Lasergraphics, Pinnacle Publishing Services, Ken DellaPenta, Bob Firkin, and British Airways. **BRITISH AIRWAYS**
The world's favourite airline.

INDEX